Sexual Violence and Sacred Texts

Edited by

Amy Kalmanofsky

WIPF & STOCK · Eugene, Oregon

Wipf and Stock Publishers
199 W 8th Ave, Suite 3
Eugene, OR 97401

Sexual Violence and Sacred Texts
By Kalmanofsky, Amy
Copyright © 2017 by Kalmanofsky, Amy All rights reserved.
Softcover ISBN-13: 978-1-7252-8895-9
Hardcover ISBN-13: 978-1-7252-8897-3
eBook ISBN-13: 978-1-7252-8896-6
Publication date 10/7/2020
Previously published by Dog Ear Publishing, 2017

This edition is a scanned facsimile of the original edition published in 2017.

The most serious and unaddressed worldwide challenge is the deprivation and abuse of women and girls, largely caused by a false interpretation of carefully selected religious texts and a growing toleration of violence and warfare.
—Jimmy Carter

We dedicate this volume to all women of faith, but particularly to those who are victims or survivors of sexual violence. Each of us recognizes the violence within our sacred texts and the violence done by them. It is our hope that this volume helps you find strength in your tradition and provides a way for you to engage with its uglier texts, and perhaps even a means to heal from them.

אז יבקע כשחר אורך וארכתך מהרה תצמח
Then may your light burst forth like the dawn, and your healing spring up quickly.
—Isaiah 58:8

Contents

Acknowledgments   vii

Contributors   ix

Introduction   1

1. How Feminist Biblical Scholarship Can Heal Victims of Sexual Violation
   Amy Kalmanofsky   9

2. "To Be One and the Same with the Woman Whose Head Is Shaven": Resisting the Violence of 1 Corinthians 11:2–16 from the Bottom of the Kyriarchal Pyramid
   Shelly Matthews   31

3. "Dipping a Finger in Honey": Sense Making in the Face of Violent Texts
   Sarra Lev   53

4. Sexual Violence and Qur'anic Resources for Healing Processes
   Celene Ibrahim   75

5. Naming Violence: Qur'anic Interpretation between Social Justice and Cultural Relativism
   Ayesha S. Chaudhry   95

6. Gang-Raped and Dis-Membered: Contextual Biblical Study of Judges 19:1–30 to Re-Member the Rwandan Genocide
   Fulata Lusungu Moyo   125

Selected Bibliography   141

Acknowledgments

Many thanks to the Carter Center for its generous grant support of FSR Books toward publication of works that are consistent with the Carter Center's activities under its Human Rights Program and its Mobilizing Action for Women and Girls Initiative. To learn more about the center's Forum on Women, Religion, Violence, and Power, visit http://forumonwomen.cartercenter.org/#.

The contributing authors and editor are grateful to Elisabeth Schüssler Fiorenza for her lifetime commitment to excellent scholarship, which addresses vital issues in feminist studies in religion. We strive to honor her legacy, and we thank her for asking us the question that galvanized our conversation and produced this volume.

Contributors

Ayesha S. Chaudhry is associate professor of Islamic studies and gender studies in the Department of Classical, Near Eastern, and Religious Studies and the Institute for Gender, Race, Sexuality, and Social Justice at the University of British Columbia. She was the 2015–16 Rita E. Hauser Research Fellow at the Radcliffe Institute for Advanced Study, Harvard University. Her research interests include Islamic law, Qur'anic exegesis, and feminist hermeneutics. She is the author of *Domestic Violence and the Islamic Tradition: Ethics, Law and the Muslim Discourse on Gender* (2014) and is currently working on two book projects, titled: "A Feminist Sharia: Re-Imagining A'isha, the Messenger of the Prophet of God" and "The Colour of God." Chaudhry earned a PhD from New York University in the Department of Middle Eastern and Islamic Studies.

Celene Ibrahim holds a joint faculty appointment as the Islamic studies scholar-in-residence at Andover Newton Theological School and Hebrew College, where she codirects the Center for Inter-Religious and Communal Leadership Education (CIRCLE). She also serves as the Muslim chaplain for Tufts University. Ms. Ibrahim is widely published and lectures frequently at universities, libraries, and museums around the United States and beyond. Her most recent publications include a chapter on Islamic family law in

Women's Rights and Religious Law: Domestic and International Perspectives (2016). She earned an MA in women's and gender studies and Near Eastern and Judaic studies from Brandeis University and an MDiv from Harvard Divinity School.

Amy Kalmanofsky is associate professor of Bible at the Jewish Theological Seminary, teaching courses on biblical literature, religion, and feminist interpretation of the Bible. Her scholarship examines the biblical representation of women and the roles women play in the Bible, focusing specifically on texts that depict sexual violation. Her first book, *Terror All Around: The Rhetoric of Horror in the Book of Jeremiah* (2008), used horror theory to examine the ways the Bible works to terrify its audience. Her most recent book, *The Dangerous Sisters of the Hebrew Bible* (2014), explores the biblical portrayal of sisters and sisterhoods and argues that both play a vital, though destabilizing, role in the Bible's narratives. Kalmanofsky earned a PhD from the Jewish Theological Seminary.

Sarra Lev is chair of the Department of Rabbinic Civilization and associate professor of rabbinic literature at Reconstructionist Rabbinical College. A member of several Jewish communities, Rabbi Lev has also taught courses on Judaism for programs and institutions, including Jewish Alive and American, the Feminist Center of the American Jewish Congress, Me'ah, New York University, and Bat Kol: A Feminist House of Study, which she cofounded. Lev's publications include numerous articles on women's and gender studies in the *Journal of Feminist Studies in Religion*, *Nashim*, and *Association for Jewish Studies Review* as well as a chapter in *The Passionate Torah* (2009). She earned her rabbinic ordination and a MHL from Reconstructionist Rabbinical College and a PhD in rabbinic literature from New York University.

Shelly Matthews is professor of New Testament at Brite Divinity School. She is the author of *The Acts of the Apostles: Taming the Tongues of Fire* (2013), *Perfect Martyr: The Stoning of Stephen and the Construction of Christian Identity* (2010), and numerous journal articles and book chapters focusing on feminist biblical interpretation. Currently, Matthews is working on a feminist biblical theology of resurrection and is coauthoring a feminist commentary on the Gospel of Luke for the Wisdom commentary series published by Liturgical Press. Her extensive service to the Society of Biblical Literature includes cofounding the Violence and Representations of Violence among Jews and Christians section, and the Racism, Pedagogy and Biblical Studies consultation. She earned a ThD from Harvard Divinity School and is an ordained United Methodist minister.

Fulata Moyo is a scholar-activist who interrogates religious resources in search of gender justice. She is the World Council of Churches' Programme Executive for a Just Community of Women and Men, and currently a visiting scholar at Harvard Divinity School. Her research and activist interests focus on how African women's storytelling and theologies inform the quest to end gender-based violence. Moyo coedited *Women Writing Africa: Eastern African Region* (2007) for the Feminist Press. Her other publications include several book chapters as well as articles on gender justice and religion in journals such as *Ecumenical Review*, *International Review of Mission*, and *Journal of Gender and Religion in Africa*. She earned a PhD from the School of Religion and Theology, University of KwaZulu-Natal, South Africa.

Introduction

At the 2014 Annual Meeting of the American Academy of Religion, the *Journal of Feminist Studies in Religion*, under the direction of Elisabeth Schüssler Fiorenza, invited six female scholars representing various faith traditions to participate on a panel addressing the topic of sexual violence and sacred texts. I was privileged to be part of the panel and the conversation that began that day and continued forward, of which this volume is a product. Our task was "to identify methods of interpretation that could engender a process of healing from sexual violence and abuse perpetrated in and through sacred scripture." Participating in the conversation with me, a professor of Hebrew Bible at the Jewish Theological Seminary, were Shelly Matthews, a New Testament professor at Brite Divinity School; Sarra Lev, a rabbinics professor at the Reconstructionist Rabbinical College; Celene Ibrahim, the Islamic Studies scholar-in-residence at Andover Newton Theological School and the Hebrew College; Ayesha Chaudhry, a professor of Islamic studies and gender studies at the University of British Columbia; and Fulata Lusungu Moyo, who is the program executive for the Women in Church and Society project under the auspices of the World Council of Churches and a research fellow at the Harvard Divinity School.

Sadly, no religion has a monopoly on sacred texts that depict, justify, or even incite sexual violence. And most of the sexual violence that falls within the purview of these sacred texts is directed against women. Each of the panelists addressed the topic from her distinct research and faith positions, but was encouraged to engender a dialogue that could look for methodological commonalties that potentially could serve as a means through which readers across faiths could encounter these disturbing texts, particularly readers who have experienced sexual violation.

It was this last expectation that caused me to hesitate before accepting Elisabeth's invitation to participate on the panel. Like my fellow panelists, I have been trained primarily as an academic. Though as a Jew I have a religious relationship with the Hebrew Bible, as an academic, I strive to approach it from an impartial perspective and to provide readings that adhere to the integrity of the Bible and the worlds that produced it. My work has focused on the Bible's most violent texts, seeking to draw attention to these texts and to understand better their function within the biblical context, but I had not considered the ways my scholarship could enable a contemporary audience, let alone people who had been victims of violence, to engage positively with these texts. Not being a therapist, I felt ill-equipped to do so. Yet after considering the invitation, I felt compelled to do so.

I share now the reasons I felt compelled to participate on the panel, because I believe they are reasons shared by my fellow panelists and because they help articulate why the essays in this volume matter and why the project we undertook could and should serve as a model of engaged scholarship. As I mentioned, sexual violence is an all too familiar part of sacred texts across all faith traditions. With the influx of women, and particularly of feminist scholarship, into the academy and the seminary, these texts have received a great deal of attention. It would be naïve to think that scholars could simply identify and interpret these texts without addressing their impact on 21st-century audiences, let alone how they can be integrated within a contemporary sacred context. The texts that each of us examine academically are very much live, sacred texts for millions of people. Even if we wanted to remain in the enclave of the academy, we could not ignore these people or their religious communities. They are our students, our students' students, and our readers.

Just as sexual violence is prevalent in ancient sacred texts, sexual violence is prevalent in contemporary society. If the statistics are right that about one in seven women have been sexually violated, those of us who are academics are more than likely teaching students who have directly experienced sexual violence.[1] The recent attention to rape on college campuses makes this even clearer. We owe it to our students at least to acknowledge if not to consider how they may be experiencing our "academic" discussion of these disturbing texts; in fact, it would be irresponsible not to. Before teaching a unit on rape texts in the Hebrew Bible, I introduce the topic a week in advance and admit that this may be a personally difficult, religiously challenging, but important topic for students to discuss. Students have expressed appreciation for my introduction, often taking the opportunity to talk with me further about their personal experiences and reactions. Of course students will encounter rape scenes in secular literature as well, and I do not think it is always necessary to prepare students before they encounter difficult or upsetting material. Yet, because the material I teach is considered by most of my students to be sacred, and many are redefining their relationship to the material, I assume the Bible's rape texts will evoke a deeply personal response, and I feel responsible for guiding them emotionally through the experience of studying these texts.

I contend that we, as scholars of sacred texts, regardless of our own religious orientations, have an added responsibility to consider the effect that texts that portray or even condone sexual violence have on our students. Though some may be beginning their paths to become scholars of the Hebrew Bible, the New Testament, the Talmud, or the Qur'an, most of our students are not being trained for the academy. For example, I teach at a Jewish seminary that educates and trains rabbis and that offers undergraduate and graduate programs

---

[1] As I mention in my contribution to this volume, rape statistics are notoriously difficult to determine. In his book *Missoula: Rape and the Justice System in a College Town*, Jon Krakauer cites a study conducted by the Centers for Disease Control and Prevention that estimates that 19.3 percent of American women have been raped in their lifetimes (Krakauer, *Missoula* [New York: Doubleday, 2015], xiii).

in Jewish studies. For the most part, my students are neither impartial nor objective. They are biased readers of the Hebrew Bible, who carry the burdens and the blessings of years of religious school education and synagogue experience, and who are working hard to develop an adult relationship with their foundational sacred texts. I can model for them objective academic standards and teach them to be critical readers of the Hebrew Bible who are aware of the biases they bring to their studies, but I also must acknowledge that what they learn shapes their religious selves and will shape the religious communities they serve or will be a part of.

In other words, my students are studying a sacred text, not a historical artifact. They want the Hebrew Bible to speak to who they are and how they live their lives. They are not willing to read the story recounted in Judges 19 (see Moyo's contribution for the full narrative) of the concubine who is gang-raped and killed and whose body is dissected into twelve pieces, simply as an ancient fable. They want to know why their sacred text includes such a brutal story, if and how they can mine this story for any meaning, and how the presence of this story influences the sanctity of the biblical canon.

These are good questions, and as scholars, we will do well to answer them and not to dismiss them as questions asked by religiously inclined, nonacademic readers. We need our lay readers, not only because they are our audience who fill our classrooms and buy our books, but also because they challenge us to justify ourselves and force us to see beyond the narrow world of academic discourse. As I mention in my contribution to this volume, scholars such as Susanne Scholz and Nancy Bowen—and all the contributors to this volume—reach beyond the academic community and look for ways that their scholarship can affect communities socially and religiously. Many of our students will contribute to and shape the communities they will be a part of or will lead. We must be responsible to them and validate their questions if not help them find satisfying answers to them.

We should feel obligated to help them integrate a text like Judges 19 into their religious lives, perhaps, co-opting Lev's language, as a text that *summons* them to be advocates against sexual violence. Doing so does not distort the meaning of the text. Rather, it enables readers to engage openly and honestly with this difficult text, and to find meaning and purpose in it. It also enables scholars who engage with the most challenging sacred texts to write and teach honestly, maintaining critical integrity while having a significant social impact. By naming the violence inscribed in our sacred texts, and by using these texts as summons to action, our scholarship can work to curb violence and to build stronger and safer communities.

The essays in this volume provide a nexus between academic and social discourse, and thereby provide a model for what I label to be engaged scholarship—scholarship that is in dialogue with and affects people's lives. All the panelists who participated in this discussion are committed to engaged scholarship. The interfaith framework of the panel also models and ensures dialogue. Clearly, each panelist addressed different texts that raised different challenges that were reflected through different faith traditions and communities. Yet, despite these differences, the commonalities amongst the panelists were starkly apparent. Not only was there a shared desire to participate in engaged scholarship, but each panelist struggled with the fundamental issue of how to read difficult sacred texts and therefore was first and foremost a *reader* who understood the power and the empowering experience of interpretation.

We all recognize the expansiveness of scripture and the multiplicity of meanings that are embedded in any text. We also understand how a text can acquire new meanings when, to use Moyo's language, it is "embodied," filtered through real lives and real life experience. In essence, each of us modeled ways of reading that could, as Matthews writes, "decenter" traditional interpretations. We are adding our voices to traditional discourse in an effort to provide new perspectives that should be perceived as a legitimate part of this discourse and that works to enhance it or, at times, as Chaudhry hopes, counter it. We understand the power of interpretation, for the impact it can have on both traditional interpretations and the interpreter. As Chaudhry observes, it is powerful to be the one who names, to be the one who interprets texts and names the violence inscribed within them. As I suggest, it is also empowering to interpret a text through the lens of one's personal perspective and experience. For those who have experienced sexual violation and who interpret sacred texts that inscribe sexual violence, the process of interpretation, I contend, can promote healing by providing women with agency and voice.

While editing this volume, what struck me most were the many questions each panelist raised. Though I could cull a much longer list, I offer a few examples. In her essay, Ibrahim asks, "How can I engage in scholarship on gender and violence in such a way that names violence but does not play into politicized attempts to emphasize the alterity of Muslims?" (p. 79) and "Can *Muslima* theology play a role in responding to—or even ameliorating—sexual violence within and beyond Muslim contexts?" (p. 93). Lev asks in her essay: "What aspects of a story do we ourselves embellish or augment in order to 'rescue' either ourselves or someone else? When do we explain away actions in order to make the mistakes look less egregious?" (p. 73). Chaudhry asks, "Why some Muslim scholars still feel compelled to follow precolonial, patriarchal, and violent readings of Q. 4:34 when they can choose to follow any of the postcolonial, nonviolent interpretations?" (p. 98). I ask, "Can feminist biblical scholarship serve people emotionally? Can it foster positive feelings of connection to the very texts that it complicates?" (p. 13).

For me, these many questions, and the willingness to ask questions, demonstrate a reflective method of interpretation shared by each of the panelists that validates the expansive nature of interpretation and challenges the belief in a fundamental meaning. As Lev notes, "if we embrace the summons, we embrace questioning" (p.74). Each of us who participated in this project understands that the process of interpretation is never static and should always be reflective, always questioning the values, choices, and objectives of the texts and of those who do the interpretation. Many years ago,

Schüssler Fiorenza introduced the concept of a "hermeneutics of suspicion," which sought to reveal the hidden biases of the texts and of their interpretations.[2] The contributions in this volume testify to her legacy. We panelists are all suspicious readers—not content or passive readers—of our sacred texts. Our suspicions of the texts we study and of those who interpret them, including ourselves, provide focus to and animate our work. We understand interpretation to be an ongoing process, and we continuously challenge our texts and ourselves as we engage in it. For myself, this process ascribes sanctity to the texts I study. For me, it is the reader's encounter with the text and the reader's struggle to find meaning within it that makes a text sacred.

Despite my initial hesitation, I am extremely grateful for the opportunity to participate in the conversation. It was a pleasure to discover and to engage with excellent scholars who do similar work to my own yet from different faith perspectives. I feel encouraged and emboldened by them. I am also particularly grateful for the challenge of extending myself beyond academic discourse by considering how my work can positively affect people. Academics rarely think in terms of "healing." As many PhDs joke, we are not *those* kinds of doctors. Yet, this project has convinced me that academics can contribute to the emotional and social health of our society, and that scholarship can matter to people outside of the academy and can be more than an intellectual exercise. Every essay in this volume matters. Every essay responds to the sexual violence inscribed in our sacred texts in order to counter the sexual violence in our society. Unable to remove the violence from our sacred texts, we strive to use these violent texts, if not to remove the violence within our society—perhaps an unattainable goal—at least to help heal those who have experienced sexual violence.

Since most of the texts readers will encounter in this volume will disturb and infuriate, I close this introduction with a biblical

---

[2] See Elisabeth Schüssler Fiorenza, *But She Said: Feminist Practices of Biblical Interpretation* (Boston: Beacon, 1992), 57.

passage of hope and healing from the prophet Hosea. After reconciling with Israel, God promises Israel in Hos 2:21–22:

> I will betroth you forever.
> I will betroth you in righteousness and in justice, with kindness and mercy.
> I will betroth you with faithfulness, and you will know YHWH.

So many of our sacred texts inscribe and justify sexual violence. Those of us who teach and study these texts, I contend, are obligated to respond to this violence. Those who have suffered sexual violence deserve justice, kindness, and mercy. I hope the essays in this volume can help them encounter their sacred texts and heal from and through the violence inscribed in those texts.

CHAPTER 1

How Feminist Biblical Scholarship Can Heal Victims of Sexual Violation
Amy Kalmanofsky

I suspect all of us participating in this discussion could engage in an interesting but horrific game of Name Your Sacred Text's Most Sexually Violent Passage toward Women. There certainly are a variety of Hebrew Bible texts to choose from. There is the story of a husband who dismembers his violated wife, in Judges 19, and a brother who rapes his sister, in 2 Samuel 13. There are also laws that subject women to shameful ordeals if the women are suspected of adultery, and those that mandate stoning if a woman is accused. Among my "most sexually violent texts" is Ezekiel 16:62-63. These are the final verses in chapter 16, the chapter in which the prophet portrays Israel as his lascivious, unfaithful wife. Ezekiel describes in this chapter how God brutally punishes promiscuous Israel in kind, exposing her nakedness before her lovers (Ezek 16:36-37), an act that indicates rape, according to Susanne Scholz and Mary Shields,[1]

---

[1] See Susanne Scholz, *Sacred Witness: Rape in the Hebrew Bible* (Minneapolis: Fortress, 2010), 182-95; and Mary E. Shields, "An Abusive God? Identity and Power/Gender and Violence in Ezekiel 23," in *Postmodern Interpretations of the Bible: A Reader*, ed. A. K. M. Adam (Saint Louis: Chalice, 2001), 136.

and commanding her lovers to stone her and pierce her with swords (Ezek 16:40).[2]

To many, my choice of passage would seem arbitrary. I could have selected any number of passages from Ezek 16 or even identified the whole chapter as my most sexually violent text. What distinguishes these verses for me from other violent texts is the way they condone violence and inscribe it onto Israel's body and her future under the guise of divine compassion and reconciliation. After having punished Israel, God promises to renew his covenant with her.[3] The passage reads: "I will establish my covenant with you and you will know that I am YHWH. So you will remember and feel shame. You will no longer open your mouth because of your shame upon my forgiving you for all that you did, says Lord, YHWH," (Ezek 16:62–63).

It is clear from this passage that Israel survived her husband's rage and that her marriage is restored because of God's willingness to forgive her. Although God accepts her back, she is forever shamed and changed. Rendered mute, Israel has lost her ability to express herself and to fight for herself. If visually depicted, her image would resemble the image used in the advertisement for the documentary film chronicling Muslim women's stories of sexual assault, *Breaking Silence*, reproduced by Ibrahim in her contribution to this volume.[4] Ezekiel's Israel has no agency. Whereas once she was a beautiful young bride (Ezek 16:10–14), she now is a woman scarred by violence, one who easily could be subject to future sexual violence. Contrite, shamed,

---

[2] Yael Shemesh argues that Israel's punishment reflects the ancient practice of punishing the offending limb. Sexually promiscuous Israel offered her genitals freely to her lovers; therefore, God exposed her genitals before her lovers (Shemesh, "Punishment of the Offending Organ in Biblical Literature," *Vetus Testamentum* 55, no. 3 [2005]: 343–65, esp. 357–59).

[3] God behaves in Ezekiel 16 like the typical "Old Testament" God alluded to by Shelly Matthews in her contribution to this discussion. Matthews makes clear that one of her goals in her essay "is to underscore that the Christian scriptures are not innocent of the ideologies that both inspire domestic violence and sanction that violence as God ordained" (p. 34).

[4] See Celene Ibrahim, "Sexual Violence and Qur'anic Resources for Healing Processes" (chapter 4).

and silenced,[5] Israel is the image of an abused woman, an image that demands an emotional, religious, academic, and political response.

According to Andrew Weaver, John Preston, and Charlene Hosenfeld, sexual assault "is the most rapidly growing violent crime in the United States."[6] The statistics are alarming. An estimated 15 per cent, or about one in seven, women report being sexually violated. Of course, this figure is difficult to substantiate and is expected to be much higher because women and men do not always report sexual violations. It is estimated that only 16 per cent of rapes are reported in the United States.[7] Another factor that makes it difficult to determine rape statistics is that it is not always clear, or agreed upon, what constitutes a sexual violation.[8]

Sexual assault is common in the Bible, and it is mostly, though not exclusively, against women. It is important to recognize that men can be threatened with sexual violation in the Bible, as Lot's guests are in Genesis 19, or be victims of sexual violence, as Lot himself is at the end of that chapter. Men also can be portrayed *as if* they were victims of sexual violence, as Scholz suggests that defeated Samson is portrayed in Judges 16.[9] Though the Bible does include these male-rape stories, stories about female sexual violation are more prevalent,

---

[5] In their handbook for clergy on sexual issues, Andrew Weaver, John D. Preston, and Charlene Hosenfeld note, "many victims, largely due to feelings of shame and guilt, never tell anyone and do not report the event to the police" (Weaver, Preston, and Hosenfeld, *Counseling on Sexual Issues: A Handbook for Pastors and Other Helping Professionals* [Cleveland: Pilgrim, 2005], 156).

[6] Ibid., 157.

[7] Elizabeth A. Rider notes, "research shows that rape is less likely to be reported than all other crimes. Women often do not tell friends or family members about being raped, let alone report the incident to the police" (Rider, *Our Voices: Psychology of Women*, 2nd ed. [Hoboken, NJ: Wiley & Sons, 2005], 469).

[8] Rider refers to a study of college students in which 15 percent indicated that they had had experiences that met the legal definition of rape and in which 12 percent experienced attempted rape, yet half of the women surveyed would not consider themselves to be rape victims. Rider asks, "Are women victims if they do not even recognize that they've been raped? And why wouldn't women know this?" (ibid., 470).

[9] Noting the use of the verb ענה, translated as rape elsewhere in the Bible, Scholz writes, "the ambiguity of the text plays a crucial role for arguing that the Philistines and Delilah attempted to 'rape' Samson. ... It is a 'rhetorical game' in which the text plays on the verb's ambiguous meaning ranging from 'humiliate' to 'force/use sexually.' The connotations of rape appear in vv. 5, 6, and 19, and the possibility of indirect sexual references can be discerned in vv. 25 and 27 when Samson is forced to 'play' or 'perform' for the Philistines" (Scholz, *Sacred Witness*, 174).

appear at pivotal moments, and have significant narrative impact. There are explicit rape narratives, such as Genesis 34,[10] Judges 19, 2 Samuel 11, and 2 Samuel 13; implicit rape narratives, such as Genesis 12 and 20, in which Abraham offers Sarah in marriage to foreign leaders;[11] and metaphorical rape narratives, such as those incorporated into the prophetic texts, like Ezekiel 16, that describe Israel as God's promiscuous wife who is punished by being sexually violated.

For the past forty years, feminist biblical scholars have drawn attention to these texts, raising questions about the values they project, their literary import, and how they have been interpreted. In crucial ways, these scholars have created what I would consider to be a feminist biblical canon of sexual-violation texts that are scrutinized constantly.[12] This volume takes us in a new direction by asking each

---

[10] Although the question whether Dinah was raped remains alive for many contemporary scholars, it does not for me. It is clear from the text that Shechem takes Dinah sexually before falling in love with her and that his actions defy Israelite marriage norms. The brothers' response also makes it clear that Dinah was sexually violated. Lyn M. Bechtel offers a contrasting view to my own in "What if Dinah Is Not Raped? (Genesis 34)," *Journal for the Study of the Old Testament* 62 (1994): 19–36. For a discussion of the root ענה see Sandie Gravett, "Reading 'Rape' in the Hebrew Bible: A Consideration of Language," *Journal for the Study of the Old Testament* 28, no. 3 (2004): 279–99. Although she perceives the anachronistic problems and urges caution, Gravett recognizes the benefits to contemporary interpreters and readers in translating the root as "rape" at times; she writes, "rape might not have existed as a legal category, but gender, class, social and ethnic preferences did. The erasure of women's voices, the suffering of a defeated nation, the humiliation of men who failed their almighty God, all peek through in this word. Women and men in these cultural settings might not understand or process their experiences in the same way as twenty-first-century persons endure rape and all of its repercussions, but using a modern word to bring these ancient texts into focus does link some common reactions in both settings—the sense of physical violation, the feelings of shame and being outcast, the loss of self and place in the culture—however different the reasons for such responses" (Gravett, "Reading 'Rape' in the Hebrew Bible," 298).

[11] One could also add the stories of the concubines Hagar, Bilhah, and Zilpah, who are made to sleep with their mistresses' husbands.

[12] Phyllis Trible, *Texts of Terror: Literary-Feminist Readings of Biblical Narratives* (Philadelphia: Fortress, 1984) could be credited for establishing the canon. See also J. Cheryl Exum's *Fragmented Women: Feminist (Sub)versions of Biblical Narratives* (Valley Forge, PA: Trinity Press International, 1994); Tikva Frymer-Kensky's *Reading the Women of the Bible: A New Interpretation of Their Stories* (New York: Schocken, 2002); Esther Fuch, *Sexual Politics in the Biblical Narrative: Reading the Hebrew Bible as a Woman* (Sheffield, UK: Sheffield Academic Press, 2000); and my own *Dangerous Sisters of the Hebrew Bible* (Minneapolis, MN: Fortress, 2014).

of us to consider through the lens of our academic and religious orientations how these texts can be read by individuals who have been sexually violated.

As a feminist biblical scholar who teaches in a liberal Jewish seminary that trains students for the academy as well as the pulpit, I am grateful for the opportunity because, though committed to a critical perspective that I maintain creates educated and honest readers of the Bible, I am also committed to a religious perspective that considers the Bible sacred and that seeks to derive meaning from it. As AyeshaChaudhry notes in her essay, "religious feminists," like myself, occupy "a difficult, if not impossible space."[13] I do not want the Bible to be a historical or sacred artifact for my students but rather a text that speaks to contemporary issues and enriches their lives. I seek to nurture in my students an intellectually sophisticated and emotionally complex relationship to the Bible. I want them to see the Bible's limitations while appreciating what it offers.

A task like the one assigned to this panel is precisely the kind of work I want to do. In essence, we are asked to consider how the intellectual endeavor of scholarship can serve people's emotional needs. Feminist biblical scholarship has helped us identify some of the ugliest parts of the Bible. It has helped us understand the nature of the violence done within these texts, as well as the violence done by the texts and their interpreters. The question facing us now is whether or not it can do more. Can feminist biblical scholarship serve people emotionally? Can it foster positive feelings of connection to the very texts that it complicates? Can it help people heal? If it cannot, its task may be complete. After perceiving the Bible's underbelly, it may be time for feminist scholarship to move on and away from this sacred text.

---

[13] See Ayesha S. Chaudhry, "Naming Violence: Quran Interpretation between Social Justice and Cultural Relativism" (chapter 5).

Admittedly, I also am daunted by the task assigned to us because I speak solely as a biblical scholar who has never been a victim of a sexual violation and therefore is not a survivor.[14] I also have no formal training as a therapist or a social worker. Though I am a rabbi, I have never had a pulpit and have not had to directly counsel someone who has been sexually violated.[15] I certainly teach students who have been sexually violated, and I train rabbis who will work with people who violate and who have been violated. My immediate concern is how I help my students, especially those who have been abused and violated, encounter sacred texts that portray sexual violation and how I train rabbis to do the same.[16] Most people assume their religion and its texts provide a safe place, an ethical and emotional safe haven they can rely upon when distressed. What happens

---

[14] The distinction between "victim" and "survivor" is an important one, as Nancy A. Naples notes: "In fact, the term *survivor* is typically reserved for those who have self-consciously redefined their relationship to the experience from one of 'victim.' This redefinition can be accomplished through a combination of influences, including personal reformulation of earlier experiences, therapeutic interventions, identification with cultural products, such as 'incest poetry' or survivor narratives, and discussions with others who self-define as survivors" (Naples, "Deconstructing and Locating Survivor Discourse: Dynamics of Narrative, Empowerment, and Resistance for Survivors of Childhood Sexual Abuse," *Signs* 28, no. 4 [2003]: 1151–85, quotation on 1151).

[15] In preparation for this panel, I read articles by rabbis, therapists, and psychiatrists who work with people who have been sexually violated. I add the following to the books and articles I have mentioned already: Judith Herman, M.D., *Trauma and Recovery: The Aftermath of Violence from Domestic Abuse to Political Terror* (New York: Basic, 1992); Marie M. Fortune and Joretta Marshall, *Forgiveness and Abuse: Jewish and Christian Reflections* (New York: Haworth Pastoral, 2002); and Garth Fletcher, Jeffry A. Simpson, Lorne Campbell, and Nickola C. Overall, *The Science of Intimate Relationships* (Hoboken, NJ: Wiley-Blackwell, 2013).

[16] Wendy S. Hesford considers the pedagogical challenges of teaching violent texts; she writes, "the introduction of works that deal with violence and trauma has the potential of triggering painful memories for some readers and viewers. One of my goals in teaching such material is to foster in students an awareness of the historical and cultural contexts that shape the production and reception of representations of violence, trauma, and resistance. This has meant developing pedagogical strategies that enable students to move beyond voyeuristic stances or modes of identification that do not enable self-reflection toward stances that prompt students to reflect on their own assumptions and the cultural scripts that structure their responses" (Hesford, "Reading *Rape Stories*: Material Rhetoric and the Trauma of Representation," *College English* 62, no. 2 [1999]: 192–221, quotation on 210).

when they discover their sacred text includes sexually violent stories?[17] What happens when an abused woman reads Ezekiel 16 for the first time and discovers, as Nancy Bowen notes, "the ways in which the Bible is not a safe space for women"?[18]

My assumption in this essay is that feminist biblical scholarship can help individuals encounter these texts and work to heal individuals who have suffered sexual violation. I suggest two ways in which this scholarship works toward healing. First, it benefits those who advocate on behalf of victims of sexual violence by raising awareness and by identifying factors that trigger, sustain, and condone the violence. Scholarship that contributes to advocacy work helps to prevent sexual violence and to provide for the needs of those who experience it. Second, feminist biblical scholarship can work therapeutically by enabling victims of sexual violence to engage with the ugliest biblical texts in ways that help them heal. Interpretation, I argue, is an empowering activity.[19] It helps violated individuals name, condemn, and resist the violence in their own lives, and more importantly, it helps them assume an agency that moves them from being victims to being survivors of sexual violation. Though I may not consider the Bible's ugliest texts to be inherently sacred, I do believe that with the perspective gained from feminist biblical scholarship, these texts can help do the sacred work of healing.

---

[17] As Sarra Lev notes in her contribution, "'Dipping a Finger in Honey': Sensemaking in the Face of Violent Texts" (chapter 3) one does not have to be a victim of sexual violation to be affected by the violence within sacred texts. I agree with Lev. Much of my scholarship grapples with the violence within the Bible, particularly against women, and coheres with the methodology proposed by Lev. For this discussion, I seek to address the specific challenges faced by victims of violence who encounter these texts.

[18] Nancy R. Bowen, "Women, Violence, and the Bible," in *Engaging the Bible in a Gendered World: An Introduction to Feminist Biblical Interpretation in Honor of Katharine Doob Sakenfeld*, ed. Linda Day and Carolyn Pressler (Louisville, KY: Westminster John Knox, 2006), 187.

[19] There may be no greater argument for the power of interpretation to empower victims than the one offered by Fulata Lusungu Moyo in "Gang Raped and Dis-Membered: Contextual Biblical Study of Judges 19:1–30 to Re-Member the Rwandan Genocide" (chapter 6).

Scholarship That Advocates on Behalf of the Sexually Violated

Scholars continue to debate the relationship between real and representational violence. The stabbing of a twelve-year-old girl by two friends who claimed they were trying to prove loyalty to Slenderman, a mythic figment of the Internet, tragically raised the issue recently.[20] Although there is no consensus whether violent images, stories, songs, or games incite violent actions, scholars agree that societal norms and attitudes influence both life and art, and are represented in both.[21] Elements that initiate violence in society shape the representation of violence in its literature; therefore, understanding the violence in literature helps us understand the violence in society, and vice versa.

Feminist biblical scholarship illuminates the ideology that shapes biblical narratives, especially those narratives that portray violence against women, as Linda Day's analysis of Ezekiel 16 illustrates:

> At its core, woman abuse is not just a concern of isolated couples but has its origins in a patriarchal system of society at large. It is dependent upon a hierarchical stratification of power, whereby men hold greater power and influence than women in general, and, in male-female relationships, the right of the man or husband to dominate the woman or wife. . . . That patriarchy is the mode of operation with regard to the Bible has long been recognized, both in terms of the hierarchical social structure of monarchical Israel

---

[20] Folklorist Timothy H. Evans discusses the issue in light of the murders in his op ed "The Ghosts in the Machine," *New York Times*, June 7, 2014.

[21] Naples advocates for a materialist feminism that recognizes the intersection between social realities and all forms of expression; she writes, "materialist feminist scholars argue for an intersectional approach and resist abstracting gender form other dimensions of social identity. . . . Talk shows, celebrity biographies, newspaper accounts, fiction, songs, poetry and dramatic presentations, survivor-generated newsletters, and research studies also inform the shame and content of survivor discourse" ("Deconstructing and Locating Survivor Discourse," 1152–53).

> and the patriarchal ideology of the biblical text itself....In Ezekiel 16 one sees quite vividly power dynamics similar to those of battering relationships, both in personal and the societal realms.[22]

Identifying and analyzing this ideology helps us understand better the world that produced the Bible. For example, after examining the ideology reflected in the biblical rape narratives, as well as in the laws legislating "rape," such as Deuteronomy 21:10-14, Harold Washington suggests that ancient Israel was a "rape culture," in which "sexual assault is viewed as a manly act and women are regarded as intrinsically rapable."[23] For Washington, rape cultures produce a rape literature that protects and perpetuates this ideology; he writes:

> These imbrications of violence and gender in the Hebrew Bible are more than just reflections of the social conditions of biblical antiquity. In this literature, gender becomes a crucial articulator of the experience of violence, and thus gendered discourse becomes a means of *producing* relations of violence and domination, authenticating a violent male prerogative that remains culturally potent into the present.[24]

Though many of us would disagree with Washington about the Bible's ongoing cultural influence, his analysis helps us identify biblical values related to gender that are shared by contemporary culture,

---

[22] Linda Day, "Rhetoric and Domestic Violence in Ezekiel 16," *Biblical Illustrator* 8, no. 3 (2000): 205-30, quotation on 212-14. I happily note that Shelly Matthews in her contribution to this volume deals head-on with a text that is often interpreted to sanction male domination.
[23] Harold C. Washington, "Violence and the Construction of Gender in the Hebrew Bible: A New Historicist Approach," *Biblical Illustrator* 5, no. 4 (1997): 324-63, quotation on 352.
[24] Ibid., 331-32.

as well as to understand the ways in which gender discourse in any culture perpetuates those values. We may no longer live in a "rape culture," but the image of the violent male remains potent today. Certainly, patriarchal ideology continues to persist, and certain types of violence are attributable to it. In *The Science of Intimate Relationships*, Garth Fletcher, Jeffry Simpson, Lorne Campbell, and Nickola Overall distinguish between two types of "intimate relationship violence:" "common couple violence" and "patriarchal terrorism." Less severe, common couple violence is initiated by both genders. Men and women are its perpetrators and its victims. In contrast, patriarchal terrorism "is carried out by men who systematically use severe forms of violence to intimidate and control their partners—these are the classic wife-beaters whose partners escape to refuges, or end up in hospital, or are sometimes killed."[25]

God's relationship with Israel as reflected in texts like Ezekiel 16 conforms to patriarchal terrorism. Thanks to feminist scholars such as Renita Weems, Gerlinde Baumann, and Linda Day, we can see that.[26] In her analysis of Ezekiel 16, Day outlines the three-stage cycle of spousal abuse and argues that God's relationship with Israel manifests all three stages. She concludes that "the profile of YHWH in Ezekiel 16 matches that of real-life batterers in significant ways."[27] As Ezekiel 16:60–61 reveals, God terrorizes Israel into silent submission and promises to restore his relationship with her, yet it is an uneasy peace. As Day observes, in stage three of the cycle of abuse, the "batterer behaves in a charming and loving manner, becoming reasonable and assuring the woman that she will not again have to suffer such an incident."[28] Wanting to

---

[25] Fletcher, Simpson, Campbell, and Overall, *Science of Intimate Relationships*, 268.
[26] Renita J. Weems, *Battered Love: Marriage, Sex, and Violence in the Hebrew Prophets* (Minneapolis, MN: Fortress, 1995); and Gerlinde Baumann, *Love and Violence: Marriage as Metaphor for the Relationship between YHWH and Israel in the Prophetic Books* (Collegeville, MN: Liturgical Press, 2003).
[27] Day, "Rhetoric and Domestic Violence in Ezekiel 16," 218.
[28] Ibid., 215.

believe this is true, the abused woman stays in the relationship. But the cycle persists. Thus, even though God reconciles with Israel, God once again could become enraged with Israel, and the cycle of violence easily could repeat.

Now that we clearly see the violence in the text and perpetuated by the text, the question remains: What do we do with this knowledge? As Bowen asks, "If a feminist perspective includes resistance to violence against women, then are we to resist the Bible?"[29] Certainly, there are feminist scholars (and lay readers) who find texts like Ezekiel 16 so repugnant, they consider them irredeemable and opt to walk away. Even the rabbis were uneasy with this chapter and did not include it among those read in the weekly synagogue service. But there are also feminist scholars, many of whom I assume have a religious orientation and consequently a mandate to remain connected to the Bible, who do not walk away. Instead, these scholars claim that engaging these violent texts raises consciousness about sexual violence within their communities and helps advocate on behalf of its victims. These scholars work to counter the "muteness" experienced by survivors, as Ibrahim notes, that is often "refracted on the communal level."[30] Though Bowen admits that some readers will reject the Bible, she offers a reading strategy that allows people to remain engaged, and works to raise consciousness within faith communities about sexual violence; she writes:

> Another strategy is to read the biblical text in the manner of confession. These difficult texts should be proclaimed and taught within faith communities. They should be treated not as paradigms to follow, though, but as part of our heritage from which to turn away in repentance as we

---
[29] Bowen, "Women, Violence, and the Bible," 193.
[30] Ibrahim, "Sexual Violence," p. 78.

confess that they reveal to us the sins of sexism, violence, and patriarchy.[31]

Similarly, Scholz applies feminist hermeneutics to biblical rape texts to ensure that they "remain an indispensable resource, a sacred witness, in the enduring task of reflecting, seeking, and understanding the sociopolitical, religious, and cultural meanings of biblical literature."[32] She hopes that her readings will help people "resist, dismantle, and oppose rape-prone assumptions, conventions, and conduct on individual and collective levels."[33]

I feel tremendous affinity toward the feminist scholars who continue to wrestle with these texts, illuminate their ideologies, and strive to educate the communities that engage with them. Though I do not think we live in a "rape culture," at least not in my privileged socioeconomic segment of the United States, I do think that patriarchal ideology persists, and that analyzing the Bible's ideology and naming the violence it engenders is important in combating the patriarchal assumptions of our culture and their consequences. Feminist scholarship has helped us do that. Still, I wonder if my continued engagement with these violent texts is not somehow complicit with the values they profess. Walking away from them may be the more ethical thing to do, yet, bottom line, I cannot walk away from the Bible as an observant Jew. I therefore wonder if my scholarship is not in service of my faith. Paraphrasing Athalya Brenner, am I salvaging the Bible from itself in order to salvage the Hebrew god

---

[31] Bowen, "Women, Violence, and the Bible," 194. Like Bowen, Trible contends that reading difficult texts can inspire repentance; she writes, "if art imitates life, scripture likewise reflects it in both holiness and horror. Reflections themselves neither mandate nor manufacture change; yet by enabling insight, they may inspire repentance. In other words, sad stories may yield new beginnings" (Trible, *Texts of Terror*, 2).
[32] Scholz, *Sacred Witness*, 25.
[33] Ibid., 211.

from himself, so I can lessen the blow to my own sensibilities?[34] Also, I wonder if I am able to do this, to remain engaged with these texts, because I have not been a victim of sexual violence and because I read them within a community that resists, dismantles, and opposes rape-prone assumptions. Does my privilege cloud my perspective? Does my faith cloud my ethics? How would I read these texts if I were a victim of sexual violation?

Scholarship That Works Therapeutically on Behalf of the Sexually Violated

In the previous section, I discussed feminist biblical scholarship that advocates on behalf of the sexually violated by acknowledging the violence, identifying its causes, and considering the ways it is perpetuated through sacred texts. This kind of scholarship does enable healing. By raising consciousness about abuse, it works to prevent further abuse and to provide services for the abused; however, it does not necessarily address the emotional needs of the violated individual, enabling a victim to encounter the biblical text. In this section, I consider how feminist biblical scholarship helps individuals who have been sexually violated emotionally encounter a text like Ezekiel 16 and enables them to find their voice, exhibit agency, and ultimately transform from victims to survivors. Once again, I acknowledge my limitations. I am neither a therapist nor a victim/survivor of sexual violence. Therefore, I cannot attest to whether the hermeneutic I suggest actually provides solace to someone who has been violated. I can only hope that it does.

---

[34] Athalya Brenner, "Some Reflections on Violence against Women and the Image of the Hebrew God: The Prophetic Books Revisited," in *On the Cutting Edge: The Study of Women in Biblical Worlds: Essays in Honor of Elisabeth Schüssler Fiorenza*, ed. Jane Schaberg, Alice Bach, and Esther Fuchs (New York: Continuum, 2004), 74.

Individuals who have been sexually violated exhibit symptoms of posttraumatic stress disorder as categorically defined by Judith Herman:

> The many symptoms of post-traumatic stress disorder fall into three main categories. These are called "hyperarousal," "intrusion," and "constriction." Hyperarousal reflects the persistent expectation of danger; intrusion reflects the indelible imprint of the traumatic moment; constriction reflects the numbing response of surrender.[35]

Victims suffer depression, fear, anxiety, and low self-esteem.[36] They also experience shame and guilt.[37] Weaver, Preston, and Hosenfeld urge clergy to be sensitive to the fact that many victims of sexual abuse anticipate "shaming and rebuke from their spiritual caregiver."[38] According to Herman, "The core experiences of psychological trauma are disempowerment and disconnection from others.[39] Recovery, then, "is based upon the empowerment of the survivor and the creation of new connections."[40] Herman notes that empowerment is the first principle of recovery. Those who work with victims of sexual violation need to restore a sense of agency so victims feel in control of their lives.[41] Carrie Doehring warns clergy not to impose systems of belief or practices upon those who seek their

---

[35] Herman, *Trauma and Recovery*, 35.
[36] See Rider, *Our Voices*, 479.
[37] Rider notes, "women who were closer to their rapist prior to the rape have the highest levels of self-blame and the lowest levels of self-concept after the rape. Women are particularly troubled when they had placed substantial trust in the man prior to the rape" (ibid., 481).
[38] Weaver, Preston, and Hosenfeld, *Counseling on Sexual Issues*, 157.
[39] Herman, *Trauma and Recovery*, 133.
[40] Ibid.
[41] It is interesting to note that women who fought their assailant report experiencing less distress afterward than women who did not. See Rider, *Our Voices*, 484. This suggests that having exercised some control during the assault alleviates feelings of helplessness.

guidance, but rather to allow victims to construct their own meaning and practice; she writes:

> Empowering victims is an essential ingredient of pastoral care ....The more victims can learn to recognize and share with their caregiver what it is like when they draw upon their religious faith and spiritual practices, the more they will be able to construct religious meanings and spiritual practices that are personally relevant and enhance a sense of their self-agency: their ability to be in charge of their lives.[42]

Feminist biblical scholarship helps restore a victim's agency through the empowering activity of interpretation. Interpretation enables healing. Just as there is a three-stage cycle of abuse, I outline a three-stage process of healing attuned with the goals and practices of feminist biblical interpretation. The first stage is an initial direct encounter with the text and with scholarship that names the violence within the text. As I mention above, feminist biblical scholars have focused their attention on the biblical texts that are the most violent toward women. Their attention bears witness to the violence inscribed in the sacred canon and, as Scholz would argue, in life.[43] According to Herman, a therapist's role is "to bear witness to a crime" and to "affirm a position of solidarity with the victim" as the victim recounts the violence.[44] Thus, feminist biblical scholars and therapists have a similar task. Day's reading of Ezekiel 16 has therapeutic value. She affirms that violence exists in the biblical text just as it exists in the lives of violated women.

---

[42] Carrie Doehring, *The Practice of Pastoral Care: A Postmodern Approach* (Louisville, KY: Westminster John Knox, 2006), 84.
[43] Scholz writes, "my goal is to provide readings of biblical rape texts that . . . present the Hebrew Bible as a 'sacred witness' to rape in the lives of women, children, and men" (*Sacred Witness*, 23).
[44] Herman, *Trauma and Recovery*, 135.

The second stage of the healing process is active interpretation. Herman emphasizes the importance of reconstructing the memory of violation into a narrative that can be integrated into the survivor's life story; she writes:

> The survivor's initial account of the event may be repetitious, stereotyped, and emotionless. One observer describes the trauma story in its untransformed state as a "prenarrative." It does not develop or progress in time, and it does not reveal the storyteller's feelings or interpretation of events.[45]

In the retelling of the trauma story, the survivor conveys her emotions and interprets her experience.[46] Biblical texts of sexual violation read like initial trauma stories. As many feminist scholars observe, they do not convey the emotional experience of the women being violated.[47] Israel never speaks in the course of Ezekiel 16; her perspective is not

---

[45] Ibid., 175.
[46] Ibid., 177.
[47] Alice Bach writes, "women do not fight back, they do not try to get away, indeed the women's struggles and pain are not narrated. Women, even the violated ones, are as silent, compliant, as uninvolved as the narrator understands them to be" (Bach, "Rereading the Body Politic: Women and Violence in Judges 21," in *Judges: A Feminist Companion to the Bible*, Second Series, ed. Athalya Brenner [Sheffield, UK: Sheffield Academic Press, 1999], 150–51).
[48] Day observes, "the first, and most obvious, characteristic of this text that one might note is that it, in its entirety is a monologue. Only YHWH speaks. . . . He describes his actions upon the woman Jerusalem, but nowhere are her thoughts or actions represented, except through his voice; all is seen only through YHWH's eyes" ("Rhetoric and Domestic Violence," 206).[45] Ibid., 175.
[46] Ibid., 177.
[47] Alice Bach writes, "women do not fight back, they do not try to get away, indeed the women's struggles and pain are not narrated. Women, even the violated ones, are as silent, compliant, as uninvolved as the narrator understands them to be" (Bach, "Rereading the Body Politic: Women and Violence in Judges 21," in *Judges: A Feminist Companion to the Bible*, Second Series, ed. Athalya Brenner [Sheffield, UK: Sheffield Academic Press, 1999], 150–51).

presented by the text.⁴⁸ Feminist biblical scholars such as Day must construct Israel's perspective, as they must construct the perspectives of all the Bible's violated women. They fill in narrative detail and add emotional content in order to tell the victim's story, as Phyllis Trible illustrates in her introduction to her groundbreaking *Texts of Terror: Literary-Feminist Readings of Biblical Narratives*, "Stories are the style and substance of life. They fashion and fill existence. . . . . In this book my task is to tell sad stories as I hear them. Indeed, they are tales of terror with women as victims."⁴⁹

A violated woman may find the example set by feminist scholars such as Trible compelling as she reconstructs her own trauma memories. These scholars' work might help her find the language to describe her experience and the strategies to interpret events and integrate them into her life. A sexually violated woman could become an interpreter herself, using her own experience to interpret texts such as Genesis 34, Judges 19, and Ezekiel 16. Giving expression to a narrative that is not her own may provide a victim with an emotional buffer and a narrative structure that could make it easier for her to express her own trauma. It also could enable her to fantasize freely about an act of violence in defense or in retaliation that she did not or would not do, providing her with what Judith Halberstam calls a "poetics of rage," an "expression that suggests that retribution in some form is just around the corner."⁵⁰ Halberstam advocates for this kind of imagined violence—the "fantasy of unsanctioned eruptions

---

⁴⁸ Day observes, "the first, and most obvious, characteristic of this text that one might note is that it, in its entirety is a monologue. Only YHWH speaks. . . . He describes his actions upon the woman Jerusalem, but nowhere are her thoughts or actions represented, except through his voice; all is seen only through YHWH's eyes" ("Rhetoric and Domestic Violence," 206).
⁴⁹ Trible, *Texts of Terror*, 1.
⁵⁰ Judith Halberstam, "Imagined Violence/Queer Violence: Representation, Rage, and Resistance," *Social Text* 37 (1993): 187–202, quotation on 196.

of aggression" that works "to destabilize the real" but not to incite actual violence.[51]

A violated woman could imagine how Israel would defend or avenge herself against God, thereby expressing how she would defend or avenge herself against her own abuser. If she wrote this fantasy down, she would be engaging in midrash, a classic form of Jewish biblical interpretation in which gaps within the text at times are filled with wildly imaginative narratives. Feminist biblical scholars use midrash to expand the perspectives included in the Bible. For example, Bowen concludes her article "Women, Violence, and the Bible" with a midrash about Tamar in Genesis 38. She portrays Tamar as an abused woman and provides her with an opportunity to express her pain and frustration, and to find solace in female companionship.[52] Responding midrashically to Ezekiel 16, an abused woman could tell Israel's side of the story, through which she could communicate her own pain and feelings of betrayal. Such midrash engenders healing. Speaking for Israel enables the violated woman to speak for herself.

The final stage of healing is when a victim is able to assume full agency of her narrative and her life. Having constructed her narrative, she owns her story and is able to assume her full voice. No longer the mute, shamed, and submissive woman, she speaks for herself. Feminist biblical scholars, such as Day, have shown how biblical women often do not have a voice. Others, such as Bowen, have provided biblical women with voices through midrash. There are also feminist scholars who hear women's voices within the biblical text itself, even when those women are portrayed as victims, and recognize their agency. In my book *Dangerous Sisters of the Hebrew Bible*, I argue that Tamar (not the Tamar of Genesis 38) talks back to her brother Amnon, both before and after he rapes her, and fights for herself in 2

---

[51] Ibid., 199.
[52] Bowen, "Women, Violence, and the Bible," 196–99.

Samuel 13:12 and 16.[53] Similarly, Tikva Frymer-Kensky contends that Bathsheba, who was sexually violated by King David, speaks up for herself in 2 Samuel 11:5, informing the king that she is pregnant so he can fix the situation and save her life.[54] Even Israel talks back to the God who violated her. Carleen Mandolfo reads Lamentations 1 and 2 as Israel's response to God's accusation and punishment recorded in the prophetic books such as Ezekiel. She sees Lamentations as Israel's "attempt to reclaim agency."[55] Applying midrashic hermeneutics, Mandolfo identifies Israel's subversive discourse in which she challenges God, telling him that her crimes were not so clear-cut and that his punishment is too severe.[56] Mandolfo considers Lamentation's Israel "the Bible's most intrepid female voice of resistance."[57] She rewrites the prophet's story, casting herself in a very different light. In Mandolfo's reading of Lamentations, Israel is no longer the villainous wife but the more sympathetic figure of the bereaved mother.[58]

Women healing from sexual violation may appreciate recognizing agency in women who fight back even if they ultimately are violated. Perhaps those who fight back function as role models of resistance, especially given the constraints placed upon them by the Bible's dominant ideology.[59] Not wanting to portray women solely as victims, feminist biblical scholars also appreciate these women.

---

[53] See *Dangerous Sisters*, 107–11.
[54] Frymer-Kensky, *Reading the Women of the Bible*, 148–50.
[55] Carleen Mandolfo, *Daughter Zion Talks Back to the Prophets: A Dialogic Theology of the Book of Lamentations* (Atlanta, GA: Society of Biblical Literature, 2007), 3.
[56] Ibid., 18, 83.
[57] Ibid., 85.
[58] Ibid., 89.
[59] Describing the prophetic worldview to which Israel responds in Lamentations, Mandolfo writes, "these prophetic texts constitute mini-master narratives in their own right. They uphold the normative worldview—patriarchal, monotheistic, and so on—of the Bible that distinguishes men from women and believers from apostates. As such, these prophetic representations do what many master narratives (unfortunately) do—they justify violence against those groups they characterize as somehow morally deficient" (ibid., 15).

We long to hear and not just to fabricate women's voices in the Bible. Feminist biblical scholars who find or construct women's voices in the Bible can help real-life women who have suffered sexual violation find and construct their voices, which is essential for their recovery. As Herman writes, a victim of sexual violation "must be the author and arbiter of her own recovery."[60]

But again, I must raise the issue whether feminist biblical scholars such as myself who perceive female agency and hear women's voices in the Bible work to justify a text that should not be justified. Does the image of enraged Israel overshadow the image of silenced Israel? Are women served better by Day's analysis than by Mandolfo's? Women (and men) may benefit physically and ethically more by exposing the Bible's violence and condemning it than by offering a counternarrative of resistance. Such counternarratives could be considered complicit in the efforts to salvage the Bible from itself, as Brenner suggests. Feminist biblical scholars who do not wish to legitimate or perpetuate violence may be better off not hunting for counternarratives within the Bible. Instead, perhaps, we should walk away.

In conclusion, I once again must own my position as a committed liberal Jew who is not willing to declare the Bible an unsafe space for women and walk away from it. Instead, I acknowledge that the Bible is not perfect, far from it.[61] It includes texts of great violence against men and women, but especially against women. We have a responsibility to own these passages. We should be honest readers who are not distracted by what is good, beautiful, or sacred but who should see what is ugly and dangerous as well. As scholars, we have the task of helping others read the Bible. Our fundamental task as

---

[60] Herman, *Trauma and Recovery*, 133.
[61] Sarra Lev writes about violent sacred text: "The text is there not to give us a view of a perfect world but to give us a view of an *imperfect* and highly human world so we may be impelled to move ourselves, and hence that world, one more step toward perfection" ("Dipping a Finger in Honey," p. 60).

educators is to help our students and readers encounter the text intellectually and emotionally. On the whole, I think we do one better than the other. We know how to explain with great intellectual precision the text and the context of the Bible for our students and for our colleagues. This panel discussion has asked us to focus on the emotional encounter, to consider how victims of sexual violation can relate to biblical texts of sexual violation, and to consider how feminist biblical scholarship can engender emotional healing.

My contention is that feminist biblical scholarship can effect healing. It can work to advocate on behalf of those who are victims of sexual violation, by witnessing the violence, by educating about its causes, and by considering how representations of violence embody and perpetuate societal norms and values that induce violence. In this way, feminist biblical scholarship raises awareness, which hopefully helps to reduce the occurrence of violence and provides support and services for the victims of violence. Feminist biblical scholarship also works therapeutically to help women reclaim their position as agents in their lives. Textual interpretation, I argue, is an empowering activity. It also can be a healing one through which a woman who is a victim of violence can become a survivor. By interpreting biblical texts of violence, a woman is able to express her feelings, engage in fantasy, construct her own narrative, and work to claim agency in her life. She certainly claims agency for herself as a reader of the Bible, and for those within the Bible who are without agency. She is able to name and condemn the Bible's violence and to give voice to the Bible's victims.

Ezekiel portrays God as angry and violent, and Israel as passive and punished. Interpretation allows feminist biblical scholars like Athalya Brenner to condemn God and the behavior he exhibits; Brenner writes:

> I regard the violent description of YHWH as a professional soldier and dissatisfied husband who tortures his "wife" as

> unacceptable, on general humanistic-ethical as well as theological and social-gendered grounds. I regard the relevant passages as pornographic and beyond salvation not only for feminists but also for any objector to violence, be that violence divine or religious or otherwise. The Hebrew god is violent.[62]

For Brenner, feminist biblical interpretation declares this portrait of a violent God beyond salvation. She may be correct. Yet, as we have seen, feminist biblical criticism not only condemns, it also saves. Carleen Mandolfo's reading of Lamentations works to save Israel by integrating her perspective and story into the Bible. It provides Israel with a voice. I have argued that Mandolfo's efforts, and the efforts of other feminist biblical scholars, can work on behalf of real-life victims of sexual violence, affirming the violence in the Bible and the violence in women's lives, and challenging us all to resist the violence. By encouraging them to become interpreters of text, feminist biblical scholarship empowers women who are victims of sexual violence. It helps them to shape their narratives, find their voices, and transform themselves from being victims of sexual violation to being survivors.

I sincerely hope that feminist biblical scholarship engenders healing, yet I have raised the possibility that the best course of action—the true path to recovery for both victims of sexual violation and for societies that continue to incite it—is to expose the Bible's violence and then to walk away from it. As a committed Jew, I am unwilling to do that. Instead, I am a feminist biblical scholar committed to rereading and rewriting the Bible's stories of sexual violation, and to helping the Bible's violated women open their mouths and find their voices. Perhaps my work and the work of others can help real women then find their voices as well.

---

[62] Brenner, "Some Reflections on Violence," 79.

CHAPTER 2

"To Be One and the Same with the Woman Whose Head Is Shaven": Resisting the Violence of 1 Corinthians 11:2–16 from the Bottom of the Kyriarchal Pyramid
Shelly Matthews

Renita Weems's pathbreaking work on metaphors of domestic violence in the Hebrew prophets begins with the provocative questions "What in the image of a naked, mangled female body grips the religious imagination? What can humiliating women and mutilating their bodies have to do with talk about God's love for a people?"[1] Engaging these questions, and questions like them, has resulted in a large and impressive body of scholarship on sexual violence by feminists specializing in the literature of the Hebrew Bible. In the field of New Testament studies, however, there is no correlative "feminist biblical canon of sexual violation texts" generating a comparable amount of scholarship, such as the one Amy Kalmanofsky identifies for the Hebrew Bible in this volume.[2]

To be sure, Christian scripture studies are not devoid of scholarship on the issue of domestic and sexual violence. Rita Nakashima Brock challenged long ago the paradigms of atonement and submission at the heart of much Christian interpretation of the sacred scriptures as sanctioning

---
[1] Renita J. Weems, *Battered Love: Marriage, Sex and Violence in the Hebrew Prophets*, Overtures to Biblical Theology (Minneapolis, MN: Fortress, 1995), 1.
[2] See Amy Kalmanofsky's contribution to this discussion for this bibliography (chapter 1).

cosmic child abuse.[3] Elisabeth Schüssler Fiorenza has addressed the issue of domestic violence directly in a few key articles, and documenting and analyzing the politics of kyriarchal submission in Christian scriptural literature linked to such violence is an ongoing concern in her oeuvre.[4] A number of studies have focused on the whore of Babylon in Revelation 17:1–8 as an image of a sexually violated woman.[5] Recent attention to the sexual violence inherent in the institution of slavery in the New Testament period has produced scholarship on this particular form of household violence.[6] These disparate studies do not add up to a sustained and comprehensive treatment of the links between sexual violence and Christian scriptures, however.

The relative lack of scholarship devoted to the relationship between Christian scriptures and domestic violence may owe in part

---

[3] Rita Nakashima Brock, *Journeys by Heart: A Christology of Erotic Power* (New York: Crossroad, 1988). See also Delores Williams, "Black Women's Surrogate Experience and Christian Notions of Redemption," in *After Patriarchy: Feminist Transformations of the World Religions*, ed. Paula Cooey, William R. Eakin, and Jay B. McDaniel (Maryknoll, NY: Orbis, 1991), 1–13.

[4] Elisabeth Schüssler Fiorenza, "Ties that Bind: Violence against Wo/men," in *Transforming Vision: Explorations in Feminist The*logy* (Minneapolis, MN: Fortress, 2011), 97–124. See also her historical documentation and theo-ethical analysis of the politics and the*logy of submission in many of her works, beginning with Elisabeth Schüssler Fiorenza *Bread Not Stone: The Challenge of Feminist Biblical Interpretation* (Boston: Beacon, 1984), 65–92, and Elisabeth Schüssler Fiorenza *In Memory of Her: A Feminist Historical Reconstruction of Christian Origins* (New York: Crossroad, 1983), 243–314.

[5] For entries into the literature and debates concerning the rhetorical effect of this image, see Jennifer A. Glancy and Stephen D. Moore, "How Typical a Roman Prostitute Is Revelation's 'Great Whore'?" *Journal of Biblical Literature* 130, no. 3 (2011): 551–69; Caroline Vander Stichele, "Remembering the Whore: The Fate of Babylon According to Revelation 17:16," in *A Feminist Companion to the Apocalypse of John*, ed. Amy-Jill Levine, Feminist Companion to the New Testament and Early Christian Writings 13 (New York: T & T Clark, 2009), 106–20; Lynn R. Huber, *Like a Bride Adorned: Reading Metaphor in John's Apocalypse*, Emory Studies in Early Christianity (New York: T&T Clark, 2007); Barbara R. Rossing, *The Choice between Two Cities: Whore, Bride, and Empire in the Apocalypse*, HTS 48 (Harrisburg, PA: Trinity Press International, 1999); Elisabeth Schüssler Fiorenza, *The Book of Revelation: Justice and Judgment*, 2nd ed. (Minneapolis, MN: Fortress, 1998), 95–96; and Tina Pippin, "The Heroine and the Whore: Fantasy and the Female in the Apocalypse of John," *Semeia* 60 (1992): 67–82.

[6] See, for example, Jennifer A. Glancy, *Slavery in Early Christianity* (New York: Oxford University Press, 2002); and Joseph A. Marchal, "The Usefulness of an Onesimus: The Sexual Use of Slaves and Paul's Letter to Philemon," *Journal of Biblical Literature* 130, no. 4 (2011): 749–70.

to a form of Christian Marcionism that implicitly—if not explicitly—relegates the problem of violence in biblical religion to the "Old Testament" God of wrath who is somehow regarded as distinct from the "New Testament" God of love. It may also be explained, as noted by Schüssler Fiorenza, by the fact that links between sexual violence and Christian the*logy are for the most part *covert* rather than *overt*:

> Christian the*logy overtly condemns oppressive forms of exploitation and victimization such as incest, sexual abuse, femicide, or rape. Nevertheless, Christian proclamation of the kyriarchal politics of submission and its attendant virtues of self-sacrifice, docility, subservience, obedience, suffering, unconditional forgiveness, male authority and unquestioning surrender to G*d's will *covertly* advocate in the name of G*d patriarchal practices of victimization as Christian spirituality.[7]

In the context of this multi-faith discussion of sexual violence and scriptures, it also must be noted that redressing the lack of attention to links between the Christian scriptures and the problem of sexual violence has relevance for contemporary Christian perceptions of Islam. As Ibrahim notes in her contribution to this volume, especially since the wars ignited as a result of 9/11, "Muslim men are understood to be uniquely inclined to commit acts of insolence and physical violence upon women and girls," and "Muslim women and girls are perceived to be uniquely or particularly vulnerable."[8] Surely, this widespread perception, in a culture with a Christian religious majority, that domestic violence pertains uniquely to Islam, is predicated on the assumption that Christian scriptures and theology do not, or could not, promote such violence.

---
[7] Schüssler Fiorenza, "Ties that Bind," 110.
[8] Celene Ibrahim, "Sexual Violence and Qur'anic Resources for Healing Processes" (chapter 4). The stereotypes that Christians hold pertaining to Islam, women, and violence contribute, of course, to the "impossible space" occupied by Muslim feminists on which Ayesha Chaudhry reflects in her contribution to this discussion.

Thus, with a thick bibliography on domestic and sexual violence in the Hebrew scriptures, on the one hand, and simplistic assumptions among Christians pertaining to violence in Islam, on the other, one of my tasks as a scholar of the Christian scriptures invited into this conversation is to underscore that this collection of scriptures is not innocent of the ideologies that both inspire domestic violence and sanction that violence as God-ordained. Both Moyo and Kalmanofsky stress in this volume the connections between recognizing the violent aspects of scripture and naming and breaking the silence pertaining to contemporary gender-based violence as a means to engender healing. Similarly, recognition of the sexual violence in scriptures is an important aspect of Lev's proposed hermeneutic of reading religious texts as a "summons" or "provocation." In a similar spirit of understanding recognition of violence as the first step in healing from violence, I devote the next section of this paper to naming violent aspects of one passage from the Christian scriptures, Paul's argument in 1 Corinthians 11:2–16 concerning the necessity of wo/men[9] who pray or prophecy in the assembly to cover their heads.[10]

---

[9] I employ the neologism *wo/men*, introduced into feminist scholarship by Elisabeth Schüssler Fiorenza, as a means of signaling that not all women are the same but differ according to class, ethnicity, race, sexuality, religion, nation, and experience. The slash also reminds that there are marginalized men in the world, and were throughout history, who face oppressions and who are also categorized as not "real" men. I employ the traditional spelling "women" in this paper when it seems necessary to underscore that the argument of the biblical passage or secondary scholarship in question is predicated on the assumption of a binary system of gender.

[10] Although many Muslim scholars have argued persuasively for the multivalence of veiling in Muslim cultures (see, for example, Homa Hoodfar, "The Veil in Their Minds and on Our Heads: Veiling Practices and Muslim Women," in *Women, Gender, Religion: A Reader* ed. Elizabeth A. Castelli, with the assistance of Rosamond C. Rodman [New York: Palgrave, 2001], 420–46), I note that in early Christian rhetoric, arguments for veiling women are built on the premise of women's subordination and inherent inferiority to men. (In addition to 1 Cor. 11:2–16, see especially Tertullian, *The Veiling of Virgins*, and Mary Rose D'Angelo, "Veils, Virgins and the Tongues of Men and Angels: Women's Heads in Early Christianity," in Castelli, *Women, Gender, Religion*, 389–419.) Thus, while I am interrogating the violence linked to arguments for veiling in this essay, I am speaking specifically within my Christian context and do not assume that veiling in other cultural and religious contexts necessarily signifies such subordination and inferiority.

Recognizing Violence in Readings of 1 Corinthians 11:2–16

I have chosen to focus on this passage from 1 Corinthians because of its central role in Christian arguments from the religious right concerning wo/men's subordination. As Gillian Townsley notes, the book commissioned by the Council of Biblical Manhood and Womanhood (CBMW) in support of its central concern for wifely submission in marriage, *Recovering Biblical Manhood and Womanhood: A Response to Evangelical Feminism*, contains more references to this biblical passage than to any other: eighty-nine total references to this passage or to verses within it.[11] Thus, for CBMW, 1 Corinthians 11 is as important to the project of subordinating women as are the household codes that directly exhort the submission of wives, slaves, and children to their husband, master, or father (Eph 5:21–6:9; Col 3:18–4:1; 1 Pet 2:18–3:7) and receives considerably more attention than the infamous passage prohibiting women's speech and authority in 1 Timothy 2:8–15.

The scholarly literature on 1 Corinthians 11:2–16 is voluminous, and the interpretation of nearly every aspect of it is widely debated.[12]

---

[11] John Piper and Wayne A. Grudem, eds., *Recovering Biblical Manhood and Womanhood: A Response to Evangelical Feminism* (Wheaton, IL: Crossways, 1991). Cited in Gillian Townsley, "The Straight Mind in Corinth: Problematizing Categories and Ideologies of Gender in 1 Corinthians 11:2–16," in *Bible Trouble: Queer Reading at the Boundaries of Biblical Scholarship*, ed. Teresa J. Hornsby and Ken Stone (Atlanta, GA: Society of Biblical Literature, 2011), 247–81, esp. 265. The Council of Biblical Manhood and Womanhood was founded in the United States in the late 1980s by leaders of Southern Baptist, Presbyterian (PCA), and nondenominational evangelical Christian churches. Their purpose is to promote a binary and "complementarian" view of gender in church and society, in which only two genders are recognized, women submit to men in marriage, and wives take up primary duties of homemaking and childcare. The book, *Recovering Biblical Manhood and Womanhood* was published shortly after the organization's founding, and in 1992, it was named Book of the Year by the evangelical Christian periodical *Christianity Today*.

[12] In addition to intense debates concerning the connotation of "head" and the obscure phrase "because of the angels," which I discuss below, debates are also waged over whether the key issue here entails veiling of the head or the proper styling of the hair (or both); whether the passage is Pauline or a non-Pauline interpretation; whether the passage is concerned with all women and men, or merely the relationship between husbands and wives; and how much importance should be granted to the directives concerning the men in worship.

Though I assume that some readings of the passage are more persuasive than others, I do not provide an expansive account of my own interpretation of the passage here. I focus in this section instead on underscoring a number of readings of the text, including those espoused by CBMW, which employ violent rhetoric against wo/men. I organize these readings around three key aspects of the passage.

(1) *Passages in which Paul lays out arguments pertaining to the question of the relationship of man to woman.* First Corinthians 11:3 proposes an argument from definition pertaining to the relationship of man to woman:[13] "But I want you to understand that Christ is the head of every man, and the husband is the head of his wife, and God is the head of Christ" (1 Cor 11:3, NRSV). The passage is convoluted and, especially within Christian evangelical circles, its meaning is highly contested. The chief point of contest is the connotation of the word "head" (Gk: *kephalē*). One the one hand, the more adamantly subordinationist Christians, represented by the CBMW, read the passage as establishing a hierarchy of headship: God-Christ-Man-Woman, and—given that the context here is concern for gender roles in worship—especially the hierarchy of man over woman. On the other hand, Christian evangelicals advocating for the equality of men and women (of whom the Christians for Biblical Equality, or CBE, are emblematic) maintain that the Greek word "head"/*kephalē* does not literally mean "ruler" or "authority over" but rather "source," in the sense of origin of, or

---

[13] Antoinette Clark Wire analyzes this and other arguments from definition in 1 Corinthians as follows: "Definition as an argument depends less on correspondence with empirical reality than on its own claim that something logically or universally has a certain character . . . but defining seldom happens where meanings are not contested, and competing definitions are at least implied. . . . Definition is a powerful rhetorical tool because it gives universal warrant to affirmative claims" (Wire, *The Corinthian Women Prophets: A Reconstruction through Paul's Rhetoric* [Minneapolis, MN: Fortress, 1990], 23–24).

temporal priority before, and then insist that "source" need not connote hierarchy.[14]

Those who read and celebrate 11:3 as establishing a hierarchy of man over woman underscore that Paul is concerned to establish hierarchy of genders by pointing to his subsequent argument for the secondary and subordinate nature of woman in vss. 8–9. These verses draw from Genesis 2 to make an argument concerning the priority of man on the basis of the order of creation: "Indeed, man was not made from woman but woman from man. Neither was man created for the sake of woman, but woman for the sake of man" (1 Cor 11:8–9, NRSV; cf. Gen 2:18–23). In contrast, those who read Paul as ultimately making an argument for the equality of women and men in 1 Cor. 11:2–16, while not disputing this argument for the primacy of man from the order of creation in vss. 8–9, insist that the hierarchical force of these verses is neutralized by Paul's subsequent concession in vss. 11–12a: "Nevertheless, in the Lord woman is not independent of man or man independent of woman. For just as woman came from man, so man comes through woman" (NRSV). According to Judith Gundry Wolf, for instance, this concession of interdependence "in the Lord" and acknowledgment of women's role in biological reproduction "cancels out the exclusive privilege of man" and "gives women equal status."[15]

---

[14] For an exhaustive exploration of the head/source debate from a historical-critical exegetical perspective, with special attention to scholarship by interpreters who identify as Christian evangelicals, see Anthony C. Thiselton, *The First Epistle to the Corinthians: A Commentary on the Greek Text* (Grand Rapids, MI: Eerdmans, 2000), 812–23. Most biblical exegetes outside of Christian evangelical circles read the "headship" text as the establishment of a hierarchy, though, distinct from the subordinationist Christian interpreters, they neither celebrate this hierarchy nor leverage it into an argument for the subordination of women in the present. See, for example, Wire, *Corinthian Women Prophets*, 23–24, 117–18; and Christopher N. Mount, "1 Corinthians 11:3–16: Spirit Possession and Authority in a Non-Pauline Interpolation," *Journal of Biblical Literature* 124, no. 2 (2005): 313–40, esp. 331–32.

[15] Judith M. Gundry-Volf, "Gender and Creation in 1 Corinthians 11:2–16: A Study in Paul's Theological Method," in *Evangelium, Schriftauslegung, Kirche: Festschrift für Peter Stuhlmacherzum 65. Geburtstag*, ed. Jostein Ådna, Scott J. Hafemann, and Ottfried Hofius (Göttingen, Germany: Vandenhoeck & Ruprecht, 1997), 151–71, esp. 162–63.

In terms of effecting violence against wo/men, the reading that interprets these passages as an argument for the hierarchy of man over woman and then celebrates that relationship as God-ordained may take pride of place. Though these arguments are not overtly advocating sexual abuse, rape, or femicide, such subordinationist rhetoric is still violent rhetoric, inscribing women as a diminished form of humanity, second to man and farther from God than man in the established hierarchy. This diminishment paves the way for more extreme acts of exploitation and victimization.

This is not to say that arguments for understanding 1 Corinthians 11:2–16 as advocating gender complementarity are free of violent effects, however. To be sure, such readings are distinct from hierarchical ones in proposing equality between the genders, yet their interest in gender complementarity shares common space with hierarchical readings of the passage, to the extent that they celebrate the passage as offering divine sanction for the existence of gender only in its binary form, male and female[16]; affirming the exclusivity of heterosexual union; and accounting for any "balance" that women achieve with men as owing to female reproductive capacity. That is, to celebrate dimorphic and fixed gender roles is to affirm heteronormativity, an affirmation that effects violence upon those who do not conform to this norm.[17]

These verses in 1 Corinthians 11:2–16 that are debated in terms of the question of gender hierarchy based on definitions of headship and the primacy of man in the order of creation are perhaps the most widely known. They are the ones that receive most attention by those

---

[16] For a critique of scholarship on gender equality in Galatians 3:28, for reifying rather than challenging the male/female dichotomy, see Dale B. Martin, "The Queer History of Galatians 3:28," *Sex and the Single Savior: Gender and Sexuality in Biblical Interpretation* (Louisville, KY: Westminster John Knox, 2006), 79–82.

[17] For documentation of hate crimes against persons within LGBTQ communities in the United States, see Stephen Sprinkle, *Unfinished Lives: Reviving the Memories of LGBTQ Hate Crimes Victims* (Eugene, OR: Wipf and Stock, 2011); and also the continued documentation on the *Unfinished Lives Blog*, http://unfinishedlivesblog.com/.

arguing for wifely submission, as well as by those who champion Paul as a proponent of gender equality in the form of a binary gender complementarity. I turn now to aspects of the passage where questions of violence against wo/men also arise and that are relevant to our present discussion, even if they do not receive as much attention among a wide readership.

(2) *The reading that understands Paul's cryptic argument concerning veiling "because of the angels" (11:10b) as a threat of sexual violence.* One of the most obscure verses in all of Pauline literature is 1 Corinthians 11:10, "For this reason a woman ought to have authority on her head, because of the angels" (NRSV, slightly modified). Many scholars attempting to puzzle out the historical rationale for this argument look to biblical and extra-biblical literature that emphasizes angelic lust for human wo/men and conclude that Paul's argument for wo/men's veiling "because of the angels" is a threat of sexual violence (see, for instance, Gen 6:2–4 and its elaboration in 1 Enoch 7). As one version of this argument casts it, in ancient ideologies of sexuality and gender, a woman's head functions metonymically as her genitals. Thus, the argument proceeds, through uncovering their heads and exposing their sexuality, the women are making themselves vulnerable to rape by the angels present in the sanctuary space who harbor uncontrollable lust. To quote Dale Martin, Paul employs here "the threat of authoritative action against [the women which] can scarcely exclude the implied threat of aggressive penetration to enforce their submission. They will be 'put in their place' by means of a super-male symbol of power: the angelic phallus."[18] To be sure, not all scholars agree that this reference to the angels carries with it these sexually violent connotations and the elaborate grounding of this argument in extra-biblical literature may not be known widely among a general

---

[18] Dale B. Martin, *The Corinthian Body* (New Haven, CT: Yale University Press, 1995), 245.

readership,[19] yet it is offered up as an explanation in a handful of study bibles and preaching commentaries.[20] Martin's particularly aggressive argument that this verse threatens sexual violence is contained within his widely cited and acclaimed monograph on 1 Corinthians and thus receives at least some hearing in divinity schools and other contexts in which academic readings circulate.

Readers who are aware of this interpretation are invited to contemplate the idea that the threat of sexual violence against wo/men pervades the cosmic sphere, where even the heavenly beings are prepared to chasten the unsubmissive with the violent force of a penetrating phallus. This reading also plays into the widespread cultural understanding that wo/men are at fault when they are raped, since they are responsible for protecting themselves from the violator's gaze, through dressing with "proper" modesty, and are culpable for their own violation should they fail to do so.

(3) *The shaming and exclusionary rhetoric pertaining to veiling and shorn heads.* Verses 5 and 6 of 1 Corinthians 11 offer up an argument from shame as rationale for veiling, along with a sarcastic imperative directed toward any wo/man resisting Paul's exhortations:

---

[19] For my own critical analysis of Martin's argument, see "*A Feminist Analysis of the Veiling Passage* (1 Corinthians 11:2-6): Who really cares that Paul was not a Gender Egalitarian after all?" Lectio Difficilior 2 (2015). Http://lectio.unibe.ch/. Others who interpret 11:10b without reference to the threat of angelic rape include Wire, *Corinthian Women Prophets*, 118–22; Jason D. BeDuhn, "'Because of the Angels': Unveiling Paul's Anthropology in 1 Corinthians 11," *Journal of Biblical Literature* 118, no. 2 (1999): 295–320; and Schüssler Fiorenza, *In Memory of Her*, 228.

[20] See, for instance, *New Interpreter's Bible*, vol. 10 (Nashville, TN: Abingdon Press, 2002), 929. The English Bible (KJV, Norton Critical Edition, 2012) annotates 1 Cor 11:10 as follows: "In light of the common Jewish conception of angels as sexually threatening (see Mark 12:25 note; Gen 6:1-4 and notes), Paul may understand veils to screen from angelic advances the women vulnerable during the spiritual openness of ecstatic worship" (361). Compare also the *Jewish Annotated New Testament*, 304. While not explicit about sexual threat, *Access Bible* (NRSV) and *New Interpreter's Study Bible* (NRSV) cross-reference Gen 6:1-4 in their notation of 1 Cor 11:10. I thank my research assistant, Anna Bowden, for her work in locating these references.

> [A]ny wo/man who prays or prophesies with her head unveiled disgraces her head—it is one and the same thing as a wo/man whose head has been shaved. For if a wo/man will not veil herself, then she should cut off her hair. But if it is disgraceful for a wo/man to have her hair cut off or to be shaved, she should wear a veil. (1 Cor 11:5–6b, NRSV, slightly modified)

The argument appeals to the worshipping community in Corinth based on an honor-shame binary: honorable wo/men are those who veil during worship; shame adheres to wo/men who do not veil in the Corinthians' assembly and to all wo/men whose hair is either shorn or cut short.

Exegetes generally agree that while the wo/men in the Corinthian assembly might resist Paul's argument that their own head-covering practices were shameful, both Paul and the wo/men in Corinth would regard shaven or cropped hair as the mark of a shamed wo/man.[21] Because gender roles are clearly at issue in 1 Corinthians 11:2–16, scholars often explain the argument from shame by pointing to instances of shorn or cropped hair in ancient texts which seem to connote wo/men who have taken up masculine practices or who have otherwise disassociated themselves from expected gender roles. As Gordon Fee notes, "the shame seems clearly to be related to her becoming like a man with regard to her hair, thus by analogy suggesting that the women were blurring male/female relationships in general and sexual distinctions in

---

[21] For instance, Gordon D. Fee, *The First Epistle to the Corinthians* (Grand Rapids, MI: Eerdmans, 1987), 510–12; Raymond F. Collins, *First Corinthians*, Sacra Pagina 7 (Collegeville, MN: Liturgical Press, 1999), 393–416; and Thiselton, *First Epistle to the Corinthians*, 828–30. For a number of ancient texts linking shorn or cropped hair to shame, see Max Küchler, *Schweigen, Schmuck und Schleier: Drei neutestamentliche Vorschriften zur Verdrängung der Frauen auf dem Hintergrund einer frauenfeindlichen Exegese des Alten Testaments im antiken Judentum* (Freiburg, Switzerland: Universitätsverlag, 1986), 78–83.

particular.²² Another possible reason acknowledged for Paul's argument that shorn heads are shameful is that such shaving practices were associated with "pagan" religious practices.²³ Implicit in the identification of these two reasons for shame—either a practice that blurs gender and sexual boundaries, or a practice of idolatry—is that the wo/man is morally culpable for the shame associated with the appearance of her head/hair.

The violence of Paul's rhetoric here, overlooked by nearly all exegetes, cuts in a number of ways. For one, the imperative "let her hair be shorn" is a sarcastic argument for some physical action to be performed upon the wo/man refusing to veil that s/he presumably does not wish to be performed. Though it is not often acknowledged as such, Paul's dismissive sarcasm is a form of violent rhetoric. For another, the assumption that it should go without saying that masculine appearance of a wo/man is shameful forecloses any sympathetic understanding of why wo/men might willingly adopt practices of

---

[22] Fee, *First Epistle to the Corinthians*, 511. As instances of shameful practices of "homosexuality" indicated by shaved or closely cropped hair, Fee cites Lucian's description of the Lesbian Megilla/Megillos (*dial. het.* 5.3); and Lucian's mention of a fugitive wife who travels with shorn hair in the company of three fugitive slaves (*fug.* 27). Compare also Collins (*First Corinthians*, 393–416), who stresses the importance of gender roles to the interpretation of 1 Cor 11:2–16 by organizing the entire passage under the subheading, "Let Men Be Men and Women Be Women." On the importance of proper hairstyle to the fixing of gender roles in 1 Corinthians and other literature, see also Caroline Vander Stichele and Todd C. Penner, "Paul and the Rhetoric of Gender," in *Her Master's Tools? Feminist and Postcolonial Engagements of Historical-Critical Discourse*, ed. Caroline Vander Stichele and Todd C. Penner (Atlanta, GA: Society of Biblical Literature, 2005), 287–301.

[23] Collins, *First Corinthians*, 409. See also Cynthia L. Thompson, "Hairstyles, Head-Coverings, and St. Paul: Portraits from Roman Corinth," *Biblical Archaeologist* 51, no. 2 (1988), 99–115, esp. 113. Thompson cites Lucian *Syr. d.* 6, which reports that those who practice the rites of Adonis at the Temple to Aphrodite at Byblos shave their heads and that women who refuse to shave are forced to spend one day selling themselves for sex in the open market. Of course, Paul would regard a practitioner of the rites of Adonis as an idolater on any grounds; still, it is interesting to note that the logic of shaming in Lucian's account does not quite parallel the rhetoric of shame according to Paul's arguments, in that it is the *refusal* to shave in a ritual context that leads to the shaming of the woman in question.

shaving or cropping hair.[24] Finally, Paul's argument that shorn or cropped hair is always a matter of a wo/man's shame forecloses any sympathetic acknowledgment that wo/men's hair might also be shorn as an act of violence against her, because shaving could be enacted upon a wife as punishment for the charge of adultery, and slaves also could be subject to the forcible shaving of their heads.[25]

---

[24] For exegetes who do read the adoption of masculine appearance by women sympathetically, see Joseph A. Marchal, "Female Masculinity in Corinth? Bodily Citations and the Drag of History," in *Neotestamentica* 48, no. 1 (2014): 93–113. Marchal, like Fee and Collins, agrees that the issue here may be that the Corinthian women were engaging in practices that would make them appear masculine, but he takes this observation in a drastically different direction, to celebrate the Corinthian women's practice of "female masculinity." See also Bernadette J. Brooten's discussion of Lucian's Megilla/Megillos in *Love between Women: Early Christian Responses to Female Homoeroticism* (Chicago: University of Chicago Press, 1996), 51–53. Also included among the reasons wo/men chose to shave or crop hair are mourning rites and to demonstrate the completion of a Nazarite vow. For an important discussion of shaving rites in ritual contexts in the Hebrew Bible, see discussion of Saul M. Olyan, "What Do Shaving Rites Accomplish and What Do They Signal in Biblical Ritual Contexts?" *Journal of Biblical Literature* 117, no. 4 (1998): 611–22. For the argument that when Paul speaks of women with shaved heads, he has in view Corinthian women who have taken Nazirite vows, see Abel Isaksson, *Marriage and Ministry in the New Temple* (Lund, Sweden: Gleerup, 1965), 160–72.

[25] Shaving of the adulterous wo/man: Tacitus speaks admirably of the tribes in Germany for their practice of shaving adulterous wo/men: "[In cases of adultery] punishment is prompt and is the husband's prerogative: her hair close-cropped, stripped of her clothes, her husband drives her from his house in the presence of his relatives and pursues her with a lash through the length of the village" (*Germania* 19.2). Dio Chrysostom heralds a female law-giver from the island of Cyprus for establishing that wo/men guilty of adultery should have their hair cut off and be made harlots (*Orations* 64.3). Compare also the ritual treatment of the hair of the woman charged with adultery in Numbers 5:18. Attestation of slave-shaving practices: In the Hebrew Bible, provisions are given for how an Israelite male may take up a slave captive as a concubine or wife, which include the shaving of the head (Deut 21:12–13). Though they are not identified as slaves, Plutarch describes a comparable marriage ritual among the Spartans under Lycurgus by which women were forcibly carried off, had their heads shaved, and then were left in a dark room to await a bridegroom (*Lycurgus* 15.30). Herodotus speaks of the use of a slave's head to send messages between political agents contemplating revolt, through a process of shaving and tattooing messages on the head (*Histories* 5.35). Apuleius describes servile workers in a flour mill as having branded foreheads and half-shaved heads [capillumsemirasi] (*Metamorphosis* 9.12). Stowaways on a ship in Petronius's *Satyricon*, wanting to disguise themselves as slaves who have been punished, have their heads shaved and branded (*Satyricon* 103). Lucian's mention of a fugitive wife who travels with shorn hair in the company of three fugitive slaves, also with shorn heads, suggests associations between cropped heads and slavery (*The Runaways* 27).

Hermeneutical Issues: Identifying Methods of Interpretation That Could Engender a Process of Healing from Sexual Violence and Abuse Perpetrated in and through Sacred Scripture

In this section I move from the identification of violent aspects of 1 Corinthians 11:2–16 to more sustained reflection on hermeneutical methods that could possibly engender a process of healing.

Recognizing Multiplicative Factors of Violation and Exclusion

Reading 1 Corinthians 11:2–16 through the lens of gender alone, without attention to the intersection of gender with other social markers, allows us to identify (consciously or unconsciously) only with the "respectable" wo/men in the passage, the wo/men in the Corinthian assembly whom Paul attempts to persuade to veil, while leaving the most marginal wo/man—the shorn one whom Paul evokes for the purposes of ridicule and exclusion—outside our line of vision.[26] Engendering a process of healing for a wider range of wo/men seeking to heal from the sexual violence perpetuated by scripture requires a wider lens.

Influenced by the work of womanist theologians who call attention to the intersecting vectors of oppression, including race, class, gender, and sexuality, and by Schüssler Fiorenza's pyramid model of

---

[26] Thus, for instance, Wire, in her truly exemplary work on the Corinthian women prophets, yet trains her eye only on the "respectable women" assumed to be Paul's primary audience for these exhortations. Consider her interpretation of 1 Cor 11:5–6: "To understand these lines it is less important to determine why a woman's having short hair was considered shameful in Roman Greece—whether short hair was the mark of slaves or prostitutes or women living like men—than it is to see how Paul uses what he considers to be an unthinkable alternative to appear flexible without giving anything away. His expectation that his challenge will be shocking *shows that the women he wants to persuade are not social outcasts with no pretentions of honor but consider themselves worthy of respect in the community*" (*Corinthian Women Prophets*, 118–19, emphasis added).

kyriarchal oppression, I suggest we employ a method of reading this passage that is attentive to *all* the wo/men evoked in this text, beginning with those at the bottom of the kyriarchal pyramid.[27] Such consideration leads us to 1 Corinthians 11:5–6, the passage that evokes wo/men with shorn or closely cropped heads, as the entry point into a reading that names and resists violence.

It seems important to recognize how the rhetoric of 1 Corinthians 11.5–6 seeks to divide wo/men into two camps—those who are honorable and those who are shameful—and then to raise questions concerning the kyriarchal dynamics that produce shame. Among the questions that could be raised here with respect to these ridiculed and dismissed wo/men are: What assumptions about gender and femininity (and/or race and/or status) result in the violent shaming of wo/men who are judged to be too masculine, and/or outside of the authority of a man?[28] What violence produces the institutions of prostitution and slavery, and how do factors of gender, race, and ethnicity intersect in these institutions, both ancient and modern? How might we challenge cultural-religious assumptions that a man has the right to inflict violent punishment on a spouse perceived as unfaithful? What links exist between violence enacted against sexual minorities and the violence that occurs in kyriarchal, heterosexual relationships?

---

[27] Delores S. Williams, "The Color of Feminism: Or Speaking the Black Woman's Tongue," *Journal of Religious Thought* 43, no. 1 (1986): 42–58; and Toinette M. Eugene, "A Hermeneutical Challenge for Womanists: The Interrelation between the Text and Our Experience," in *Perspectives on Feminist Hermeneutics*, ed. Gayle G. Koontz and Willard M. Swartley (Elkhart, IN: Institute of Mennonite Studies, 1987), 20–28. For one discussion of kyriarchy, see Elisabeth Schüssler Fiorenza, *Wisdom Ways: Introducing Feminist Biblical Interpretation* (Maryknoll, NY: Orbis, 2001), 118–24.

[28] For the linking of cropped hair with both slave status and "Spartan" ethnicity, see Lucian, *The Runaways* 27.

Insofar as the passage attempts to shame wo/men who do not conform to feminine gendered behaviors and/or heterosexual marriage, readers might resist by naming and celebrating wo/men, both in ancient and contemporary contexts, who engage in gender-bending practices and who identify as lesbian, transgendered, masculine, or queer.[29] Insofar as the passage invokes wo/men whose heads have been forcibly shaven as punishment for the crime of adultery, or as a signal of a debasement in the case of a slave, readers might push against the grain of Paul's rhetoric to call out the violence of this force. In order to provide a broader rationale for such resistance and reading against the grain, I turn to outline a second hermeneutical approach to this text.

Decentering Paul

A hermeneutical method for resisting oppressive rhetoric in Pauline epistles, employed by a number of feminist biblical scholars, has been to shift the focus of interpretation away from the voice of Paul alone and to the voices of those with whom Paul deliberates. This method operates on the principle that the Pauline epistles are not oracles of G*d but rather are rhetorical arguments composed as an attempt to persuade a community to accept a particular point of view. On the principle that Paul's rhetoric is persuasive only if he has properly gauged the views of those with whom he deliberates, it becomes possible, through rhetorical criticism of his arguments, to reconstruct the views of others in Pauline communities. Thus, Paul's voice is decentered, becoming only one of many voices within the communal deliberations of the assemblies, and wo/men are also

---

[29] Compare with Marchal, "Female Masculinity in Corinth"; and Brooten, *Love between Women*.

imagined as participants in developing the teachings and traditions of the assemblies, traces of which are embedded in the epistles.[30]

In this method, which "places the locus of theologizing in the interaction of Christians in the assemblies," rather than in Paul's mind, contemporary interpreters are invited "to bring [their] own questions and priorities into the discussion," to weigh them against the voice of Paul and also against other voices in the Corinthian assembly.[31] With respect to 1 Corinthians 11:2–16, readers could be invited to reflect not just upon Paul's arguments as he defines proper gender relations in hierarchical and binary terms, threatens angelic violence, and dismisses wo/men whom he regards as shameful. They could also consider the ancient wo/men in Corinth, who resisted these arguments based on their experience of having been raised in Christ.

As best we can reconstruct the perspectives of the Corinthian wo/men prophets whom Paul attempts to persuade, they appear to have experienced being baptized into Christ as effecting the abolishment of social distinctions based on gender, ethnicity, and status as pronounced in the pre-Pauline baptismal formula of Galatians 3:28.[32] Whereas Paul wishes to stress that the abolishment of these

---

[30] Classic essays on decentering Paul include Elisabeth Schüssler Fiorenza, "Pauline Theology and the Politics of Meaning," *Rhetoric and Ethic: The Politics of Biblical Studies* (Minneapolis, MN: Fortress, 1999), 175–79; Wire, *Corinthian Women Prophets*; Cynthia Briggs Kittredge, *Community and Authority: The Rhetoric of Obedience in the Pauline Tradition* (Harrisburg, PA: Trinity, 1998); Cynthia Briggs Kittredge, "Rethinking Authorship in the Letters of Paul," in *Walk in the Ways of Wisdom: Essays in Honor of Elisabeth Schüssler Fiorenza*, ed. Shelly Matthews, Cynthia Briggs Kittredge, and Melanie Johnson-DeBaufre (Harrisburg, PA: Trinity, 2003), 318–33; and Melanie Johnson-DeBaufre and Laura S. Nasrallah, "Beyond the Heroic Paul: Toward a Feminist and Decolonizing Approach to the Letters of Paul," in *The Colonized Apostle: Paul Through Postcolonial Eyes*, ed. Christopher Stanley (Minneapolis, MN: Fortress, 2011), 161–74. See most recently Anna Miller, "Not with Eloquent Wisdom: Democratic *Ekklésia* Discourse in 1 Corinthians 1–4," *Journal for the Study of the New Testament* 35, no. 4 (2013): 323–54.
[31] Kittredge, "Rethinking Authorship," 332.
[32] Wire, *Corinthian Women Prophets*, 122–28. That Paul is resisting an egalitarian reading of Galatians 3:28 in Corinth is recognized not just by feminist biblical scholars; see, for instance, BeDuhn, "Because of the Angels."

social distinctions is reserved for a time in the future at Christ's parousia, the Corinthian wo/men imagine that time already initiated at baptism. Thus, they prophesy and pray in worship with heads uncovered as a sign of the abolishment of these social distinctions. If the social pressures for veiling in the presence of angels are anywhere near as strong as scholars such as Martin imagine, we are justified in celebrating these women as remarkably courageous to have resisted these social pressures in their worship practice. We may also imagine that Paul's arguments for veiling were not well received and were certainly not the last word on the matter. This can be inferred from Paul's acknowledgment at the close of this pericope that some in the congregation will "be disposed to be contentious" (Gk: *philoneikos*, "victory loving") with regard to the argument Paul makes (1 Cor 11:16).

Imagining these wo/men who were "victory-loving," confident in their own theological insights and thus in resisting Paul's violent rhetoric might assist in the process of healing from violence and abuse perpetuated through sacred scripture, insofar as these wo/men are regarded as allies and role models from the past. Imaginative reconstruction of the voices of wo/men in Corinth might enable contemporary women to also find voice. Of course, the ability to take up the Pauline epistles, imagining the *opponents* of Paul as one's allies, requires an expanded view of which voices within the scriptures are authoritative.[33] In recognition that not all violated wo/men, who turn to the Pauline epistles for healing, might be drawn to methods of interpretation that foreground voices in this text other than Paul's own, we turn finally to a method of resisting the violent rhetoric of 1 Corinthians 11:16 that draws on the words of Paul himself.

---

[33] As Kittredge wryly notes, in distinction to the model of decentering Paul proposed by feminist interpreters, the model that assumes Paul's authority and centrality "has in its favor the whole history of Western theological tradition since the Reformation in which Paul has been a source of doctrine and a heroic person who could be admired and imitated" ("Rethinking Authorship," 327).

Reading Paul against Paul

Because the method of decentering Paul proposed above is a nontraditional means of ascribing authority to biblical texts, it may be recognized that at least some wo/men who seek healing through Christian scriptures would not find this method of reading scriptures compelling. The enormous weight of authority granted to Paul's voice in Christian history and tradition is difficult for some to cast off;[34] thus I suggest one final hermeneutical method for resisting the violent language of subordination, shaming, and exclusion within 1 Corinthians 11:2–16: drawing on other passages within the Corinthian correspondence that reflect Paul's voice but subvert the hierarchy of these particular verses.

Though 1 Corinthians 11:2–16 establishes hierarchies and presumes fixed binaries of man-woman and honor-shame, I suggest that *Paul himself* offers in the first chapters of this letter a more profound understanding of the "reordering of power effected by Jesus's resurrection."[35] This reordering of power destabilizes and arguably abolishes the categories of shame and honor, weakness and power, foolishness and wisdom. As Paul meditates on the revelation of the divine in Christ crucified in 1 Corinthians 1:18–29, and on his own debased status in 1 Corinthians 4:10–13, he proclaims that G*d empowers the shamed and works through the debased—what he

---

[34] See, for instance, Schüssler Fiorenza's discussion of the "tenth roadblock" in *Wisdom Ways*, 71–74. In a final rereading of the contributions of others in this conversation, I am struck by and in sympathy with Lev's clarification that "the methods [she] is proposing are not meant to use scripture to promote healing for women who have undergone sexual violence." Rather, she is proposing "a way to heal *from* the sexual violence perpetrated by *the scriptures themselves* on their readers, be they victims of sexual violence themselves, or not" (p. 56). Perhaps it is because of my own teaching contexts, which have always been in locations where the dominant voices of scripture take on such enormous weight for many wo/men, that I attempt to offer one reading *with* the grain of the text, rather than *against* the grain, as a possible resource for consideration in our project.

[35] Cynthia Briggs Kittredge, "Feminist Perspectives: Reconstructing History and Resisting Ideologies," in *Studying Paul's Letters: Contemporary Perspectives and Methods*, ed. Joseph A. Marchal (Minneapolis, MN: Fortress, 2012), 121.

calls the "rubbish" of the world—to spread good news. He writes, for example, "has not G*d made foolish the wisdom of the world?" (1 Cor 1:20b); "G*d chose what is foolish in the world to shame the wise.... G*d chose what is low and despised in the world to shame the strong, things that are not, to reduce to nothing things that are" (1 Cor 1:27–28); and "we have become like the rubbish of the world, the dregs of all things, to this very day" (1 Cor 4:13).

Mainstream interpreters of Pauline epistles, who tend to identify with Paul, generally celebrate this reversal of power and abolishment of hierarchical categories when they are pondering the circumstance of Paul himself and his reflections on wisdom in 1 Corinthians 1–4. The celebration of the profundity of these words in Anthony Thiselton's commentary on 1 Corinthians 1:27–29 might serve as representative of this line of interpretation: "God is no human construct, called in to legitimate human power interests, but the very reverse. His love for the nobodies and **the nothings** discounted as nonentities and as **insignificant** in the value systems of the world puts the world to **shame** by its reversal of judgment."[36] Yet these interpreters continue to identify with Paul as they represent and affirm his arguments for hierarchies and worldly standards of shame in 1 Corinthians 11, without reflecting on the tension between these two modes of argumentation.

In line with countless traditional Christian exegetes, those seeking healing through scriptures from sexual violence and abuse may affirm that Paul proclaims a G*d who reverses and/or abolishes hierarchies and who values and empowers those at the very bottom of the world's order of values in 1 Corinthians 1–4. In a second step, with 1 Corinthians 1–4 placed alongside 1 Corinthians 11, it might be possible to read Paul *against* Paul. Thus, it could be recognized that G*d's reordering and empowering celebrated in 1–4 should by extension also apply to the "nothings discounted as nonentities" whom Paul attempts to shame and exclude in the latter chapter,

---

[36] Thiselton, *First Epistle to the Corinthians*, 184 (bold in the original).

beginning with the wo/man whose head is shorn and including all of the wo/men violated in 1 Corinthians 11 through the assertion of subjugating hierarchies and threatening sarcasm.

Privileging 1 Corinthians 1–4 as a lens through which to read 1 Corinthians 11:2–16 in the interest of healing requires some care. When pointing to Paul's message of the inversion of values revealed in the proclamation of "Christ crucified," it is important to stress that the wisdom of G*d is not revealed in the suffering of crucifixion itself—which would be akin to reifying and glorifying such suffering. The inversion of values lies, rather, in G*d's solidarity with those who suffer, and G*d's vindicating and healing restoration of such persons. Read this way, Paul's more profound insights in 1Corinthians 1–4 concerning God's reordering of power for the sake of an expansive love receive the recognition they are due, and his more oppressive rhetoric is named and set aside.

CHAPTER 3

"Dipping a Finger in Honey": Sense Making in the Face of Violent Texts
Sarra Lev

In his March 14, 2014, speech in Atlanta, Supreme Court Justice Antonin Scalia commented, "the Constitution is not a living organism. It's a legal document, and it says what it says and doesn't say what it doesn't say."[1] In contrast with Scalia's view of the Constitution, in Jewish tradition, it *is* common to refer to both the scriptures and the Talmud as living texts. I have come to understand this not only as a comment about permission to interpret these texts according to societal shifts but also as the *charge* to interact with them. In light of that, I have begun to think of these texts not as holy texts but as *texts in search of holiness*. As they live and breathe, they seek holiness as we do, and it is in the interaction of the reader and the text that this holiness can be found—not as definitive answers to difficult questions, but as a quest.

Many of us have spent years formulating and reformulating ways of dealing with difficult texts. We have tried apologetics, historicizing the texts, situating them within a certain class and agenda, rejecting pieces, rejecting the whole, reinterpreting, and

---

[1] "Justice Scalia: 'Constitution Is Not a Living Organism,'" *Associated Press*, March 15, 2014.

rewriting, to name just a few techniques. I don't wish to discount these, and yet the problems with them have been laid out countless times.² To my knowledge, there is no seamless solution to the endless problem of what we do with these texts that belong to us, that we are unwilling to step away from and yet are so very troubling to us.³ However, I want to present here a way of reading that has helped me grapple with some of the issues. In order to do so, I will begin with several traditional Jewish interpretive strategies that have contributed to this mode of reading and to my own search for meaning.

First, it is an oft-quoted tradition that *the Torah has "seventy faces"*⁴—that is to say, religious texts can have multiple (and sometimes conflicting) interpretations, some of which have been revealed and some that have yet to be revealed. Moreover, we are enjoined by the sages of the first two centuries of the common era to "mix it around and mix it around, because everything is in it."⁵ While leaving the tradition open in this way, a second interpretive tradition understands that *sometimes we must say "I don't know."*⁶ One finds in many commentaries the closing words "and this is difficult" (אישק), "this needs investigation" (צריך עיון), or "I don't have an explanation for this, and indeed it is very surprising (יניא דאמ אלפומ רבד אוהו רבסה דכל עדוי).⁷

---

² For example, they were eloquently outlined by Aysha A. Hidayatullah in her paper last year on this panel. See Aysha A. Hidayatullah, "Feminist Interpretation of the Qur'an in a Comparative Feminist Setting," *Journal of Feminist Studies in Religion* 30, no. 2 (2014): 115–29.
³ See, in particular, Amy Kalmanofsky's paper "How Feminist Biblical Scholarship Can Heal Victims of Sexual Violation," in which she addresses this issue throughout (chapter 2).
⁴ The word *Torah* traditionally is used to include the Talmud as well, the Bible being "the written Torah" and the Talmud being "the oral Torah." Numbers Rabbah, 13:15.
⁵ mAvot, 5:22.
⁶ Compare with Celene Ibrahim's comments on Muslim interpretive tradition in "Sexual Violence and Qur'anic Resources for Healing Processes" (chapter 4).
⁷ See, for example, Maimonides commentary on mBekhorot 8:2.

A third interpretive tradition understands the role of interpretation to be *reconciling the texts with our own sense of truth*.[8] Jewish tradition has consistently employed commentary in order to resolve discrepancies between what scripture seems to say and what we "know" to be true. For the early rabbis, this was achieved through midrash. For example, when scripture ordered the stoning of a rebellious son, the rabbis "knew" that this iron-handed decree could not possibly have been the divine intention; thus, they interpreted their way around that particular injunction by creating so many parameters that the punishment could never actually come to be.[9] Likewise, the Tosafists of the twelfth to fifteenth centuries "knew" that the Talmud must be consistent and explained how it *was* so, even when it appeared not to be. For others, this reading strategy meant (and still means) making sure that the law matches the values and norms of the current religious community.[10] This has always been

---

[8] Because this panel is only a slice of an overarching project in Comparative Feminist Studies of Sacred Texts, I want to take seriously Karen Pechilis's questions in last year's panel about integrity in this project and state outright that I write this paper not to propose a mode of scholarship in rabbinics but to propose a new hermeneutic. See Karen Pechilis, "Devotional Subjectivity and the Fiction of Femaleness: Feminist Hermeneutics and the Articulation of Difference," *Journal of Feminist Studies in Religion* 30, no. 2 (2014): 99–114. I want to differentiate here between "scholarship" and "interpretation," and emphasize that this paper is about *interpretation*. Interpretation, in Judaism, is a tradition of coming to terms with difficulties in the text. It has its own set of rules, which are quite different from those of scholarship. Whereas scholarship might claim a certain level of objectivity (with postmodernist- and standpoint-theorist caveats included), Jewish interpretation claims none, takes liberties with the texts, and recognizes that the interpretive conversation is itself a part of the process.

[9] For example, the word *son* precluded stoning a girl, or a boy who was over a certain age, because the word in Hebrew also implies childhood. Likewise, however, a child cannot be held legally responsible. This left a very short span of time (past childhood, yet not an adult) in which one could fall into the category of a "rebellious son."

[10] For example, changes to the prohibition on teaching women Torah (*Sefer Hasidim*, 313; *Ma'yanGanim*, Venice: 1553, 5:10; quoted in *Torah Temimah* on Deut 11, "and you shall teach them to your children," note 48); *Likutei Halakhot* on *Sotah*, chap. 3, pp. 21–22). See also changes to the definition of "deafness," Rabbi Moshe Feinstein (Even Haezer 3:33, etc.); Rabbi Shlomo Zalman Auerbach (Minchat Shlomo1:34, etc.); Rabbi Eliezer Waldenberg (shu't Tzitz Eliezer, 15:46, etc.); and Rabbi Yitzchak Yaakov Weiss (Minchat Yitzchak 2:113, etc.). So too, the famous injunction against polygamy by Rabbeinu Gershom (*Shulchan Aruch, Even ha Ezer, Hilchot Piryahu Reviyah*, 1:9–10).

and will continue to be the job of interpretation. Finally, I have already mentioned the reading strategy in which *text is a living tradition*, but added to this is the fact that *commentary is also part and parcel of the living tradition*. Commentaries on rabbinic texts span centuries, and although they are not considered the texts themselves, neither are the texts read without them.

Based on these principles, I want to suggest a way to read these texts, with the caveat of "this needs investigation." This essay grew out of a proposition for a panel, convened by Elisabeth Schüssler Fiorenza, seeking to compare and contrast feminist methods of interpreting texts on violence in the three monotheistic religions. The panel was invited by Schüssler Fiorenza to identify methods of interpretation that could engender a process of healing from sexual violence and abuse perpetrated in and through sacred scriptures. I want to state at the outset that the methods I propose are not meant to use scripture to promote healing for women who have undergone sexual violence. Rather, what I am proposing here is a way to heal from the sexual violence perpetrated by the scriptures themselves on their readers, be they victims of sexual violence or not. As readers of these texts, we experience their violence (all the more so if we have been victims of violence), and I believe it is imperative for us to avoid having our holy scriptures re-victimize us each time we read them.[11]

This method rests on the work of those who came before me, especially those who have developed theologies and hermeneutics of liberation—those who have spoken to issues of justice, equality, and healing. These scholars and theologians have taught us to pay a different kind of attention by asking ourselves a multitude of questions. Why is this story told at all? Why is it told in this way? What are its explicit or implicit messages? Who is it meant for and who does it

---

[11] It is compelling to me to think about how we might be able to achieve this in a community context and not just as individual readers, as with Fulata Lusungu Moyo's work with contextual Bible study. See "Gang-Raped and Dis-Membered: Contextual Biblical Study of Judges 19:1–30 to Re-Member the Rwandan Genocide" (chapter 6).

ignore? Who does it sanction, promote, affirm, or abet? Who does it reject, ignore, oppress, misrepresent, or wound? These are the questions that liberation theologies have taught us to ask, and each particular theology answers in its own way.[12]

In these theologies, however, the difficult and painful parts of scripture must often be ignored or explained away in order for God to remain, at God's core, benevolent and liberatory. In contrast, the methodology I suggest moves the emphasis to a different location. Rather than consider scripture as the *source* of an emancipatory or liberationist message, this methodology considers scripture a *call* to examine and liberate ourselves and to identify those areas of privilege that prevent us from liberating others; therefore, though some of the questions may overlap, their purpose often diverges. In particular, the method begins with the work of Schüssler Fiorenza, who has advocated and developed over the years a way to apply a "hermeneutics of suspicion" to the scriptures, which "seeks to explore the liberating or oppressive values and visions inscribed in the text by identifying the androcentric-patriarchal character and dynamics of the text and its interpretations."[13]

---

[12] As I understand it, black theology traditionally sees the Bible as a (potentially flawed, and white) human finger, pointing us back to the original (nonwhite) God, whose primary concern is liberating the oppressed. James Cone says, "God is whatever color God needs to be in order to let people know they're not nobodies, they're somebodies" (interviewed by Barbara Reynolds, *USA Today*, November 8, 1989, 11A). Black theology joins liberation theology in claiming God as the liberator, and names God's main function as the protection of the downtrodden. Process theology sees God as ever-growing and -becoming, in direct relationship to the world, while at the same time seeing God as eternally good. David Ray Griffin writes that "Process philosophy supports liberation theologians in locating the reality of God's presence and creative activity in this world" (Griffin, "Values, Evil, and Liberation Theology," in *Process Philosophy and Social Thought*, ed. John B. Cobb and W. Widick Schroeder, Studies in Religion and Society [Chicago: Center for the Scientific Study of Religion, 1981], 185). Compare with Shelly Matthews's treatment of the ways in which we, the readers, are drawn to identify with the "respectable" over and against the marginal ("To Be One and the Same with the Woman Whose Head Is Shaven: Resisting the Violence of 1 Corinthians 11:2-16 from the Bottom of the Kyriarchal Pyramid," chapter 2).

[13] Elisabeth Schüssler Fiorenza, *But She Said: Feminist Practices of Biblical Interpretation* (Boston: Beacon, 1992), 57. See also Elisabeth Schüssler Fiorenza, *Bread not Stone: The Challenge of Feminist Biblical Interpretation: With a New Afterword*, 10th anniversary ed. (Boston: Beacon, 1995), 15-16.

What I ask in this essay is how we move from recognizing those dynamics to healing from them. And if the text is a living document, then I must also ask myself how I can help it to find the holiness that it seeks, and how it can help me to do the same. As feminist readers of the text, we need not consider only the commentaries of those who have traditionally claimed ownership of these religious texts but can ourselves assert the necessity and claim the right to add to those commentaries. If we follow the tradition of reading text along with its commentary, ours becomes an additional indispensable tool without which the text cannot properly be understood.[14]

Few would claim that we have already uncovered the seventy faces of the Torah, and so I propose what I believe is an as yet unexplored method of following the injunction to "mix it around and mix it around." Let me explain. When we open a Superman comic book, we know *how* we are meant to read it, simply because it is a comic book. We do not read it as history, or as law, or as a religious text. So too, when we open a history book, we expect an account of something that "actually" took place, as flawed as we now understand that account to be. If we open a satire, we will not read it as a tragedy, even if those same words might be read as a tragedy in another setting. The same is true for any text we read.[15]

---

[14] See Judith Plaskow, "Foreword," in *Torah Queeries: Weekly Commentaries on the Hebrew Bible*, ed. Gregg Drinkwater, Joshua Lesser, and David Shneer (New York: New York University Press, 2009). This does not preclude Hidayatullah's comments about where our traditions locate religious authority ("Feminist Interpretation of the Qur'an") and Ayesha Chaudhry's excellent demonstration of the ways in which feminist commentary is outside the bounds of what "counts," whereas Da'esh is not ("Naming Violence: Qur'anic Interpretation between Social Justice and Cultural Relativism," Chapter 5). In spite of the fact that Jewish interpretation is extremely flexible, who has the right to engage in it and whose interpretation is accepted by which communities also remains quite rigid.

[15] Yann Martel's *The Life of Pi* (New York: Harcourt, 2001) plays on this, using a narrator to tell an autobiographical story that seems impossible to believe.

But what would happen if we were to read a text as if it belonged to a different genre?[16] What happens to these violent texts, for example, if we read them as satire? As poetry written in the voice of an abused woman? As horror? The moment we change the assumed genre of the text, we transform the entire text, without ever modifying, apologizing for, or excluding a word. Without a doubt, each of these enterprises is a task worth undertaking, and each would undoubtedly yield pearls of wisdom; however, in this essay I am interested in concentrating on a genre that, as yet, I am not sure has been created.

The genre I would like to explore here might be called "summons," or "awakening," or "spark," or "agitation," or "provocation."[17] The genre assumes that the text is not passively telling us a story of how things were or how they ought to be but is there to actively rouse us to become more holy.[18] If a feminist hermeneutic is about fostering justice and ending oppression based on gender, race, ability, and the like, then any text we read must not only console us, or even liberate us, but must also push us to investigate our own complicity in dynamics that perpetuate these patriarchal injustices, and provoke us to take action.

Each of us as a reader belongs to multiple identity groups, whether we recognize ourselves as members or not.[19] I am white; a Jew; a lesbian; queer; to all appearances, currently able-bodied; and middle class, to name just a few. Some identity groups fall into the

---

[16] The method I propose here does not preclude a strong command of the texts and a strong command of theories of feminism, queer studies, postcolonialism, race, and so on. These texts start out with depth that can only be drawn upon using close reading, historical context, and a command of language that allows for a multiplicity of possible readings.

[17] For the purposes of this paper, I will primarily use the term *summons*, but any of the terms is an appropriate description of the type of reading that I am proposing here.

[18] This genre may be my own invention (though I would be happy to know if it already exists).

[19] See Angela Ferguson, "Intersections of Identity: Navigating the Complexities," *Forum on Public Policy Online*, 2007, http://forumonpublicpolicy.com/papersw 07.html#multicul.

category of privileged, and others of oppressed. At any particular time, these may shift or intertwine, depending on the situation in which we find ourselves. When read as summons, holy texts require us to inhabit multiple identities simultaneously: those imbued with power and privilege, those of the powerless and oppressed, and those that shift between categories. In each of these identities, we require liberation, as James Cone writes in describing the vision of Martin Luther King Jr.: "blacks would not only liberate themselves from the necessity of bitterness and the feeling of inferiority toward whites, but would also prick the conscience of whites *and liberate them* from a feeling of superiority."[20] Read as a summons, as a story that is able to push exactly those buttons that need pushing, the religious stories that seem so violent might draw us into asking questions about our own life choices as privileged and as oppressed, as victim and as perpetrator, as a composite and messy combination of factors in a society that is rarely straightforward.

But how does this help us *heal* from the violence of the text? To begin with, by reading the text as summons, we are no longer confined to understanding it as either descriptive or prescriptive; the text is there not to give us a view of a perfect world but to give us a view of an imperfect and highly human world so we may be impelled to move ourselves, and hence that world, one more step toward perfection. We can thus expect imperfection from these texts. In fact, we must expect imperfection, but imperfection that serves a purpose. In addition, the very fact that the text is there to challenge us to grow allows us to take action. Rather than finding ourselves victimized by the text, we are educated and empowered by our interaction with it. We are not passive recipients but active participants. Finally, in reading the text as a living document, the active role that we play here

---

[20] James H. Cone, "Black Theology in American Religion," *Journal of the American Academy of Religion* 53, no. 4 (1985): 755–71, quotation on 762 (emphasis added). See also Celene Ibrahim's paper in this series, in which she presents a parallel teaching from the Sahih of al-Bukhari (chapter 4).

becomes more than just a self-reflection. Through our action, we also move the text to a different place. Each time we engage with the text, we create further commentary, and that too, in the tradition of Jewish commentary, becomes part and parcel of that living text.

Although this system may be very well and good in theory, how might it work in practice? What is necessary in order to read a text as belonging to the genre of summons? Let me take an example that has been addressed by other feminist scholars in various contexts.[21] It appears in the Babylonian Talmud, the primary object of traditional Jewish study and the primary source from which Jewish law is derived. The passage I wish to examine follows a lengthy discussion of the mechanics of sex with a three-year-old girl and the effects (or lack thereof) on her virginity. The Talmud introduces the following story:[22]

> Our sages taught: [There is] a story concerning a woman who came before Rabbi Akiva. She said to him, "Rabbi, I was 'laid' before I was three years old. What is my status with regard to [marrying into] the priesthood (*ma ani la-kehunah*)? He said to her, you are fit for [marrying into] the priesthood (*k'sherah at la-kehunah*). She said to him, "Rabbi, I will tell you a parable: to what can this be compared? To a

---

[21] See, for example, Tal Ilan, *Silencing the Queen: The Literary Histories of Shelamzion and Other Jewish Women*, Texts and Studies in Ancient Judaism (Tübingen, Germany: Mohr Siebeck, 2006), 185–88; and Judith Hauptman, *Rereading the Rabbis: A Woman's Voice* (Boulder, CO: Westview, 1998), 92–94.

[22] Please excuse the lewd language of the translation. The use of the word "lay" is the only way I have found of expressing sex in the rabbinic sense of the word. The English "to have sex with" implies a mutuality. A quick look in the thesaurus presents the following synonyms for "have sex with": be intimate, breed, copulate, fool around, fornicate, go all the way, go to bed with, have sexual intercourse, have sexual relations, mate, procreate, sleep together, fuck, lay, and screw. Only the lewd terms fuck, lay, and screw can be used to express a subject-object relationship. For the rabbinic authors of this story, however, sex (whether consensual or not) is an act performed by one person on another. This is true also of the Roman culture in which they were situated. See, for example, Craig A. Williams, *Roman Homosexuality*, 2nd ed. (New York: Oxford University Press, 2010).

baby whose finger they dipped into honey. The first time and the second, [the baby] howls at it. The third [time] he sucks it." He said to her, "if so, you are disqualified from [marrying into] the priesthood." He saw the students looking at each other. He said to them "why is this problematic in your eyes?" They said to him, "just as the entire Torah was taught to Moses at Sinai (*halakhah le-Moshe mi-Sinai*), so too [the law that] a girl under the age of three years [who has been laid] is permitted to [marry into] the priesthood was taught to Moses at Sinai." And even Rabbi Akiva only said that [she is disqualified from marrying into the priesthood] in order to sharpen [the minds of] his students.[23]

The story begins with several assumptions that we must lay out before beginning any analysis. The first is that sex with a three-year-old girl is nowhere prohibited in rabbinic texts (though that is not to say that it is encouraged). Second, sex with a girl under three years and one day does not render her virginity compromised. The rabbis believed that the hymen would grow back if the sex occurred before this age.[24] Third, there is no legal prohibition against a priest marrying a woman (or girl) on the basis of her having *enjoyed* sex.

Upon reading this Talmudic tale, certainly some of our first reactions might be nausea, rage, and, ultimately, a desire to utterly reject the text—and perhaps all the more so for those who are survivors of rape. And of course, all of those are understandable and justified reactions to so many elements of this story, in particular if we read them as many of us have been taught to understand them, as the word of God (whatever that might mean for us individually). When

---

[23] bNid 45a.
[24] This is the main concern when this topic is raised in the Babylonian Talmud. Put differently, the rabbis' question is whether the sex is to be considered sex, given that the girl's hymen grows back.

we read "holy" texts, our usual response is to judge the characters and the stories, be it positively, negatively, or both at once: We *must* believe what our holy texts say or we *cannot* believe what our holy texts say; the story is God's word and therefore tells us how things "ought to be." The values reflected by the story are antithetical to ours and therefore must be rejected. Whether we embrace or renounce the texts, we already "know" where we stand in relation to them and in relation to the world. From such a point of entry, however, we perpetuate the text's violence, whether we adopt it or reject it. We allow the text to have the power over us. We accept that it is prescriptive of behavior and that its assumptions are normative.

Having established the need to move beyond these initial judgments, the next part of this essay does just that, engaging in the exercise of reading the above text as summons. I am by no means saying that we must suspend our judgment of behaviors depicted in the texts. Quite the opposite. We must interrogate the texts. This requires examining each and every behavior of each and every character in the text. It obliges us to evaluate the choices of the narrator and the redactor of the text. In all of these cases, our judgment of the text is essential. But the summons also requires us to pick up that judgment and carry it forward to good use. The process is always dialectical, moving from the text to ourselves and back again. Much as satire offers us a way to critique society and to see society from a different vantage point, summons offers us a way to critique ourselves, to see our own beauty and our own flaws, so we ourselves may continue to grow and become.

Hearing the Call

Whether we find a story difficult or comfortable, the story calls us to learn from our response—What is it about the way a character is acting or speaking that I am struggling with? Do I recognize any of that in myself? What situation is provoking my response here? Does the character have anything to teach me about this? Do I feel comfortable with how a character is acting or speaking? What reader/listener might *not* feel comfortable with that same character? What does that character ignore that I might also have ignored, had I not considered this? What do I have to learn about myself in a parallel situation?—but before we can hear this call, we must first be willing to listen.

I am reminded of a poem by Yehudah Amichai:

The Place Where We Are Right

> From the place where we are right
> flowers will never grow
> in the spring.
> The place where we are right
> is hard and trampled
> like a yard.
> But doubts and loves
> dig up the world
> like a mole, a plough.
> And a whisper will be heard in the place
> where the ruined
> house once stood.

To hear these texts as a call for awakening, we must first be ready to be awakened—dug up, by doubts and loves—even, or especially, if that means that we may be wrong or that there are seventy potential "rights." If the characters are flawed in their humanness, then so are we. Of course, for each text, there are as many possible "right" readings and answers to these questions as there are people studying them;[25] thus, in no way could I hope to cover even the tiniest portion

---

[25] I am not suggesting that there are not also what I would consider poor readings, merely that there are multiple potentially "good" readings.

of responses. I will, however, give a few short examples of how reading this text as summons might function here.

The Call of Rabbi Akiva

Much like the multitude of narratives in which men come before the rabbis with legal cases on which the rabbi then rules, here a woman comes before R. Akiva with a case on which he then rules. She, however, does not accept his ruling, and challenges him. Moreover, the language that she uses to do so is profoundly rabbinic, calling upon the hermeneutic of the allegory and challenging an established rabbi at his own game. Rabbi Akiva's role in this text is complex. He responds from his position of power not only by attending to what she says but also by changing his ruling in accordance with her objection. Moreover, his final ruling is not even in accordance with rabbinic law (which the students point out to him)! This is not necessarily the response that we as readers might have expected from R. Akiva. What were his motivations? Did he cede his power (and ego) to a woman? Did he think he was punishing her for challenging him by ruling in accord with her own stricter claim rather than his original more lenient ruling (saying, essentially, "Fine! Have it your own way!")? Did he perhaps pick up on and facilitate the woman's tacit wish *not* to wed? Or was he (as the narrator's final comment claims) merely testing his students with this legal inconsistency?

Of course, while we attend to R. Akiva's response, we must also attend to what he omits entirely—any condemnation of the events she has reported took place when she was a girl. He does not investigate how she came to be "laid" on at least three occasions by a man when she was a small child. He offers no surprise, censure, or consolation. He trusts and acts upon her profession that she enjoyed the sex. Did he or did he not consider the wider implications of ignoring her professing publicly of having enjoyed the sex? Did he consider the woman herself? Did he consider her story, beyond its legal implications, or was he so engaged with the legal question that he failed to notice what was at stake? Did he perhaps choose not to engage her publicly about the circumstances but to approach her at some later time? Was he concerned lest a deeper, more personal, question might throw her off her game?

Each of these possibilities offers us a different call. When might *we* have overlooked or ignored what lies behind a particular "technical" question? When is it appropriate for us to say something personal in public, and when must we act as if we have not heard what lies behind the question? When have we favored not engaging with the personal? Under what circumstances does our responsibility to a system override our ability to investigate what we personally might consider injustices, even if the wider world accepts them as normative? What is our responsibility as a leader and as a representative of a particular system, be it as a rabbi in the name of a religious tradition, a politician in the name of a party line, or even a parent in the name of "proper behavior"? Each of these falls within the myriad questions that, if we read the text as summons, the figure of R. Akiva calls upon us to ask ourselves.

The Call of the Students

The students in the story respond to R. Akiva's ruling with surprise but do not directly confront him. Rather, they silently regard each other, "passively" demonstrating their discomfort. Only when R. Akiva himself confronts them do they explain that the law as they know it does not forbid this woman to marry a priest, whether or not she enjoyed the sex, as long as she was three years old or under when it occurred. The students' censure is not focused on what we would consider the abhorrent sex act itself or on their teacher's attitude (or lack thereof) toward it. That element of the story, in fact, goes entirely unnoted. Rather, they are concerned that he has failed to enact the law as they know it.

The role of the active bystander is one we seldom consider. The students' behavior in the story summons us to consider our role when we are positioned between a greater authority and the ultimately powerless. In our case, the students in this case *do* speak out against R. Akiva's ruling, though only after he calls them to account for their exchange of glances. In the case of the Babylonian rabbis, opposing another's ruling was heavily intertwined with issues of shame and social status, and thus questioning their teacher should be considered no small act.[26] In addition, the brazenness of the students in this story stands out, as what they object to is R. Akiva's *legal ruling*—probably the most risky confrontation possible in this milieu. The students offer us a successful stand of courage in the face of an authoritative pronouncement. We are called by this text to examine our own bravery when confronted by what we see as an improper use of power, even if our own relationships with those in power are at risk.

At the same time, there is another summons here, inspired by the students' failure to respond to R. Akiva's blatant lack of attention to the problematics of sex with a child. What causes this failure? Judging from their courage in confronting R. Akiva on his ruling, it does not seem to be fear that prevents them from raising an objection to the possibility of sex with a three-year-old girl. Are they so conditioned by the norms in which they are educated that the grievous harm caused by those norms becomes invisible? Is it their own insensitivity? Their avoidance? Are they resentful of the woman who has managed to manipulate the ruling of their teacher? Do they wish to penalize her? To support her? Are they ignoring her completely, in order to focus on their one and only concern—Jewish law? In the case of these students, their issue was a legal one, but the summons of this text is certainly not

---

[26] See Jeffrey L. Rubenstein, *The Culture of the Babylonian Talmud* (Baltimore, MD: Johns Hopkins University Press, 2003).

limited to a confrontation based on legality. As the bystanders, we may find ourselves in a place of privilege but not necessarily of authority. This text also calls on us, therefore, to reflect upon our choices regarding whom we notice and include in our daily consciousness. It summons us to examine the ways in which we ourselves have been educated so as to ignore certain injustices or those who are affected by those injustices. It summons us to ask how we benefit from our ignorance, and whom it behooves us not to notice.[27]

Because the text does not supply enough information about the reason for their silence, however, in the approach I am suggesting, the text also summons us to notice when we speak out. Our choices of whom and what we notice may or may not determine for whom we are willing to speak out. How invested we are as participants in, rather than executors of, a system of laws/norms and behaviors might play a part in these decisions. The fear of authority, what we stand to gain by remaining silent, how we are educated to act in a particular environment, how we envision our own power, how much we question what we are conditioned or taught to believe—each of these might have determined the students' choice to speak out against sex with a three-year-old or might determine our own choices to speak out against injustices that might otherwise remain unaddressed or unnoticed.

The Call of the Unnamed Woman

The unnamed woman in the story comes to R. Akiva with a question. She was "laid" before the age of three, and she would like to know her status with regard to marrying into the priesthood.[28]

---

[27] On this, see Eve Kosofsky Sedgwick, *Epistemology of the Closet* (Berkeley: University of California Press, 1990), 4–8.
[28] A priest is forbidden to marry a woman who has had intercourse with someone forbidden to her either through an incestuous relationship or for a number of other reasons. In this case, the text assumes that the perpetrator was forbidden to the three-year-old girl for one of these reasons (but *not* because she was a mere child).

From the outset we notice that her question expresses no censure of the story she relates—having been subjected to sex as a three-year-old child. After R. Akiva declares his ruling that she is fit to marry into the priesthood, she pushes further, seemingly unwilling to accept his declaration of her purity in light of the fact that she enjoyed the sex. She thus positions herself as even stricter about her "impurity" than R. Akiva himself, introducing a factor into the calculation that is not taken into account in rabbinic laws of purity—enjoyment. The unnamed woman imposes her own personal "law of purity" on herself, going far beyond the restrictions of rabbinic law.

It bears repeating that the basis upon which she declares her hesitation to accept R. Akiva's opinion is that she came to enjoy that rape when she was three. Her parable lays out the fact that although the first and second "laying" may not have been pleasurable, by the third time, she had grown to enjoy it. She compares it to honey, used to depict the sweetest of the sweet. The implication is that for a girl of three, sex can be as sweet as honey. Not only that, but she goes so far as to say that although the first and second times were *not* pleasurable, they *too* were like honey. In those cases, they were simply honey that she (or the infant) had *not yet discovered* was sweet.

The unnamed woman in this story is depicted not as a challenger of the system but as "one of the team." She does not come to R. Akiva to right an injustice that was perpetrated on her, by holding the rapist (for that is surely what we must call him under these circumstances[29]) accountable for his actions. Indeed, she does not

---

[29] I recognize that terms such as *rape* and *violation* may be an imposition of a value system that is absent from the text itself. I am proposing, however, a hermeneutic that both recognizes and confronts that but does not exclude the anachronism from its interpretive framework. If this text is meant to summon us, then we must accede to it speaking to our present situation, even if that situation may have been perceived differently when and by whom it was written.

even seem to notice that a violation has occurred. She does not come to R. Akiva to challenge this system that (at best) does not censure that sex, or even to ascertain the legality of such an act under rabbinic law. Rather, she comes to R. Akiva to inquire whether, *within the laws of the system*, she is "pure enough" to marry a priest. By asking this question, she cedes authority to R. Akiva and, by implication, to the rabbinic system. Through her question, she actively participates in a discourse that sanctions male possession of the virginity of girls and women, and male investment in the sexual status of nonvirginal women. Not only does she collaborate with a system that sanctions her victimization, but her parable also perpetuates the myth that nonconsensual sex, in this case even with a three-year-old girl, is as sweet as honey for its mark.

What's more, the narrator leaves us with the feeling that the woman engages the rabbis not with a dilemma that she is experiencing ("I wish to marry a priest. May I?") but with a purely theoretical question ("What is my status with regard to the priesthood?"). Does the narrator imagine an actual priest waiting in the wings to marry her? Is she merely proving her own legal prowess, asking a theoretical question that gives her a space on the floor of the rabbinic academy? Could this text present us with a story in which the hidden background is a woman promised to a priest she does not wish to marry? Does she come before R. Akiva believing that he will not sanction the marriage, at which point she is disappointed in the ruling? Is she using the system to avoid the marriage? Does she need to reject R. Akiva's ruling because his ruling has not given her what she needs in order to take control of her own life?

Within this reading, we might be called to examine when, for example, we perpetuate a system by using it for our own gain. When do we act in ways that get us what we want while reinforcing or replicating what must be eradicated? A capable woman acts meek, helpless, or ignorant before a man. A man takes the salary that is offered him without comment, knowing that his female colleague is making less. We live in a world in which we cannot avoid participating to some extent in unjust systems, but can we participate consciously, being careful to cause the least amount of damage possible and taking care not to leave those in power with the impression that the system is, in fact, working for everyone?

Alternatively, consider a reading in which the unnamed woman is so entrenched in a system that is oppressive that she is not able to see outside of it. She is the fish who is unable to recognize water. Her sense of self has been deadened, and she is emotionally desensitized to the injustices perpetrated against her. In this way, she becomes entirely complicit in the rabbinic enterprise, perpetuating the myth that nonconsensual sex of any kind, and especially with a child, can be enjoyable for the victim, and participating in a discourse that not only does not question this "fact" but uses it to discuss male possession over the virginity of girls and women.

If we read this anecdote thus, as a parable for our own lives, as a story that is able to push precisely those buttons that it *does* push, it forces us to ask some questions about our own life choices. In what ways, for example, are we complicit in our own oppression or in the oppression of others? When do we participate in (or even initiate) seemingly banal conversations in which a burning issue or dangerous assumption is being ignored? When do we repress our own pain for the sake of the technicalities that must be "dealt with in the moment"? When do we allow ourselves to be co-opted into a discourse that has the potential to hurt others or to delegitimize or ignore their pain?

The Call of the Author/Narrator/Redactor

An analysis of the narrative and redactional layers of this story is beyond the scope of this essay, but there are, again, several directions that such an analysis might take when reading this text as summons.³⁰ One might, for example, focus on the *telling* of the story, in this case the choice of specific characters (Why a woman? Why R. Akiva?) or the narrative gloss at the end of the story. Consider the narrator's choice to deploy a woman as the story's main spokesperson. The story presents a woman who has gone through the experience of sex with a man when she was three, enjoyed it, and embraced the system that sanctions it to the point that she is presented as beholden to it for deciding her future. By choosing a female character, the narrator can depict that sex from the point of view of that little girl as honey-sweet. Having heard such a description from a woman, that is, there can now be no question of its truth value. The choice of the narrator himself, like the choices that the characters make, can be understood to summon us to examine ourselves and to raise certain questions about our own choices.³¹ This story might raise questions about how we ourselves deploy people in our own storytelling when we want to make a rhetorical statement. Do our statements gain legitimacy depending on from whom we maintain we heard them? Do we seek to support our opinions or ideas by declaring them the opinions of certain people rather than others? How does this deployment affect the people or groups of people we "use" rhetorically? How might it affect those we choose not to use? What constitutes our sources of legitimization, and why?

---

³⁰ Though these texts were once mined for historical evidence, it is now commonly accepted that they are of narrative value, rather than historical accounts. Jacob Neusner, *Method and Meaning in Ancient Judaism*, Third Series, Brown Judaic Studies (Chico, CA: Scholars Press, 1981), 185–213; and Jeffrey L. Rubenstein, *Talmudic Stories: Narrative Art, Composition, and Culture* (Baltimore, MD: Johns Hopkins University Press, 1999), 3–5.

So too the intriguing suggestion of Shelly Matthews that we "decenter" the narrative or authorial voice (in her case, Paul), and "shift the focus of interpretation away from" the speaker to the spoken to. This is yet another layer that could be put into play with my methodology. See "To Be One and the Same with the Woman Whose Head Is Shaven: Resisting the Violence of 1 Corinthians 11:2–16 from the Bottom of the Kyriarchal Pyramid" (chapter 2).

³¹ I use the gendered pronoun here advisedly.

The narrative gloss at the end of the story might also summon us. The students' challenge to R. Akiva is entirely legitimate. The narrative gloss essentially "rescues" R. Akiva from seeming to have made a legal error so that we, the audience, are not left in doubt as to his legal expertise. The narrator also balances out the response of R. Akiva to the unnamed woman, with the rabbi's lack of response to his own students. When the unnamed woman challenges him on his ruling, he changes it, even though there is no legal basis to that change. When his students, however, challenge him on his turn-around, R. Akiva is unresponsive and the story is left hanging. The narrator must fill in a conclusion that explains to us why R. Akiva would make the choice to change his opinion for the unnamed woman but not for his students, who raise a faultless legal challenge. The narrator's "rescue" of R. Akiva might prompt us to ask a different set of questions: What aspects of a story do we ourselves embellish or augment to "rescue" either ourselves or someone else? When do we explain away actions to make the mistakes look less egregious? Whom do we choose to rescue, and whom do we allow to appear in all their humanness? Why do we make those choices, and whom do they serve?

Aside from narrative choices, there are several other directions one might pursue to read the narrator/redactor as summons. One might, for example, query the *placement* of the story—in other words, its inclusion in the context of a legal discussion of sex with a three-year-old girl and its implications on virginity.[32] Or, just as one examines the characters included in the story (as many have already pointed out), one might look at those whom the story does not include. The potential for finding that which summons us as readers to examine ourselves is unending.

---

[32] All of these layers interact with one another as well as functioning individually, and it is sometimes difficult to ascertain whether these issues concern a single person making these choices or a combination of people, perhaps even over vast time spans.

If we embrace the summons, we embrace questioning. As I said when I began this essay, the key to this type of reading is not in finding answers but in raising more and more questions, both of the text, and, through that, of ourselves. What I have discussed in this essay are only a few of the possible "seventy readings" of this story, and each of those readings contains many possible calls, depending on who we are and how we responded to the text on any given occasion. The idea here is neither to rescue the text nor to condemn it but to be in relation with it, pursuing our own growth, and thus the growth of the text itself. What I have presented here offers a way to loosen ourselves from the grip that the texts have had on us as feminist interpreters, and to take back that text in our own interpretive framework, as have all those interpreters who precede us. It allows us to reestablish ourselves (with the living text) as active participants in changing ourselves, the religious tradition, and (dare I say it) society at large. Without ignoring parts of the text, and without contextualizing or apologizing for it, we are able to read it not as normative or prescriptive but as a gift. Through this hermeneutic, we need not agree with the content. In fact, the content is there to *provoke* us to disagree, to think. It is there as a critical *summons* to us to continue to grow and change, as an *agitation* that gets us out of bed, an *awakening* as to who we are, and a *spark* that lights our way forward.

CHAPTER 4

Sexual Violence and Qur'anic Resources for Healing Processes
Celene Ibrahim

Sexual Violence and the Intersections of Media, Activism, and Identity Politics

In her recent appeal on the crowdsourcing website Kickstarter, Nadya Ali, journalist and aspiring documentary filmmaker, a recent graduate of Barnard College, attempted to raise funds for her feature-length documentary on Muslim women's stories of sexual assault entitled Breaking Silence.[1] The experiences of the women range from abuse by family members to gang rape. As Ali told the Huffington Post, it is in part the "culture of impunity" for perpetrators of sexual violence that she hopes to counteract by helping to bring stories to light and engender communal conversation.[2] In conversation with the editors at

---

[1] "Sexual Assault in the Muslim Community—Documentary," *Kickstarter*, accessed January 10, 2015, https://www.kickstarter.com/projects/1776612453/sexual-assault-in-the-muslim-community-documentary. As of September 2016, the film is in the final stages of postproduction. This initiative is not to be confused with a similarly themed initiative entitled "Break the Silence against Domestic Violence," founded in 2011, which was organized by recent college graduate and assault survivor Kristen Paruginog.

[2] "Four Brave Muslim Women Break the Silence around Their Sexual Assaults," *HuffPost Religion*, September 16, 2014, http://www.huffingtonpost.com/2014/09/16/muslim-women-breaking-silence-sexual-assault_n_5830640.html?utm_hp_ref=religion.

AltMuslimah, a pioneering forum run by a team of women of diverse backgrounds and dedicated to exploring gender-related issues in Islam, Ali explains that she "wanted to find a way to open the community to these issues so that some suffering can be assuaged."[3] As the film's title suggests, the messaging around the film highlights the lack of communal conversations and communal resources on this issue. As one survivor relates in the film's trailer: "Silence for me was the easiest person to talk to because silence understood I didn't want to be judged." The line is later picked up in the documentary's visual advertising campaign pictured below.

Breaking Silence advertisement on *AltMuslimah*, November 28, 2014.

---

[3] "Breaking Silence," *AltMuslimah*, November 18, 2014, http://www.altmuslimah.com/2014/11/breaking-silence/.

This fear of the consequences of bringing sexual violence to light is a common experience for many survivors, as Amy Kalmanofsky highlights in this volume in her discussion of Ezekiel 16:62–63 and its implications for rendering Israel shamed and mute. The ability to express the pain of violation is also at the core of Fulata Lusungu Moyo's turn to the story of the Levite's concubine in Judges. Moyo discusses the corpse of a sexually violated and murdered Rwandan woman, as well as her own experience of violation, as a way of "breaking the silence" around oppression and bringing to life "current living stories that are often suppressed in the conspiracy of silent shame" (131). With a comparable urgency, Ayesha Chaudhry calls attention to the "power and responsibility in naming violence as religious feminists" (118), even if it requires entering an impossible ideological terrain.

The weight of the burden of breaking silence should not be primarily upon survivors and those identifying as feminists, but certain barriers inhibit honest communal discussion. A simple anecdote can demonstrate several of those barriers. Recently, a male Muslim student came to me, in my role as a Muslim university chaplain, inspired by the grassroots nature of the *Breaking Silence* campaign. He was invested in working for positive change on this issue, and together, we suggested to the Muslim Student Association's board to include a call for support of the documentary in the weekly e-newsletter. Our suggestion met with reticence, as some of the student leaders noted the documentary's potential to feed already potent and often vitriolic stereotypes about Muslims. These student leaders, quite astutely, feared that considerable work they had already put into campus initiatives to provide nuance around Islam and experiences of being Muslim would be significantly undermined by calling attention to this documentary. The suggestion to highlight the documentary on group-run social media platforms was dropped. I relate this simple example to highlight how the shame and muteness experienced in the first order by survivors is then refracted at the communal level, perhaps especially when minority or socially marginalized communities are involved.[4]

The *Breaking Silence* documentary also raises important questions about voyeurism and the dynamics at play when women of socially marginalized identities relate their sexual experiences.[5] Ali's stated ambition with *Breaking Silence* is not to further stigmatize and emphasize alterity of Muslims in the American context, yet speaking about sexual violence in Muslim communities readily does just that. For instance, consider the most visible graphic of the documentary's funding campaign (see image above). A silhouette of a woman in a headscarf appears with a frightened look about the eyes and bearing the words "breaking silence" in place of a mouth. The graphic signals a particular way of looking female and Muslim while using the charged image of the headscarf to stand in for a complex religio-cultural identity. The image plays into underlying stereotypes that women in headscarves are distinctly disempowered, vulnerable, and unable to come to speech.[6]

---

[4] See Chaudhry for a thorough discussion of identity politics involved when entities such as "the West" and "Islam" are depicted as oppositional and Muslim actors are pressured to take sides between religious identify and the values of secular liberalism ("Naming Violence," chapter 5).

[5] For a discussion about the discursive production of Muslim girls' sexuality—and the impetus for its surveillance by others and women themselves—see Shenila S. Khoja-Moolji and Alyssa D. Niccolini, "Producing and Surveilling Muslim Girls' Sexuality: A Discursive and Affective Analysis of Young Women's Confessional Writings," in *Expanding the Gaze. Gender, Public Space, and Surveillance*, ed. Robert Heyman and Emily Van der Meulen (Toronto: University of Toronto Press, 2016).

[6] In the Qur'an, veiling is not depicted as a symbol of women's submission to men but as a protective measure to help guard women against sexual abuse. For instance, the Qur'an states, "Those who trouble/assault (*yu'dhūna*) faithful men and women undeservedly, certainly bear the guilt of slander and flagrant sin. O Prophet! Tell your wives and your daughters and women of the faithful to draw closely over themselves (*yudnīna 'alayhinna min*) their chadors (*jalābībihinna*) [when going out]. That makes it likely for them to be recognized (*yu'rafna*) and not troubled/assaulted (*falāyu'dhayna*)" (33:58–59). The Qur'an presents a very different pretext for covering than the one presented in 1 Corinthians 11:2–16, as Matthews notes (see footnote 10, pg. 34).

This tension brings me to a slippery yet productive question that guides my hermeneutical approach: How can I engage in scholarship on gender and violence in such a way that names violence but does not play into politicized attempts to emphasize the alterity of Muslims?[7] From another direction, as a *Muslimah* theologian and as someone inspired by colleagues across religious identity lines, could I identify Qur'anic resources that resonate with survivors beyond the subset of people for whom the Qur'an *already* has resonance? Hence, I attempt to highlight communal resources for preventing and responding to sexual violence within—and beyond—distinctly Muslim contexts. I consider first and foremost resources for survivors of violence; however, I also consider ways to "help" perpetrators. I understand this double-sided approach to be distinctly Islamic; a well-known teaching suggests that in confronting oppression, it is not sufficient to provide help only to the one who is victimized:

> Allah's Apostle [Muhammad] said, **"Help your brother, whether he is an oppressor or he is an oppressed one."** People asked, "O Allah's Apostle! It is all right to help him if he is oppressed, but how should we help him if he is an oppressor?" Allah's Apostle said, **"By preventing him from oppressing others."**[8]

---

[7] This tension is taken up at length in Chaudry's article in this volume ("Naming Violence," chapter 5).
[8] Adapted from Muhammed Muhsin Khan et al., *The Translation of the Meanings of Sahih al-Bukhari: Arabic-English Sah h al-Bukh r*, Vol. 3, Book 43, no. 624 (Cairo: Darussalam Publications, 1997). Available online through the Center for Muslim-Jewish Engagement at the University of Southern California, http://www.usc.edu/org/cmje/religious-texts/hadith/bukhari/. A similar version appears in other hadith collections.

Qur'anic Stories of Attempted Sexual Violence

The Qur'an does not narrate any explicit episode of sexual violence against women. It does, however, narrate two instances of attempted sexual assault, including a sexual assault by a woman on a prophet of God and an attempted sexual assault by a mob on angels. The stories provide rich grounds for deriving resources to support sexual-assault survivors at the individual and communal levels.

Power, Social Hierarchies, and Testifying against an Assailant

The story of Joseph's encounter with the wife of the Egyptian vizier has a similar plot line as the narrative in Genesis 39, although, like other stories of biblical prophets, the Qur'anic narrative carries its own style and emphasis. The story is narrated by an omniscient narrator (God), whose voice interjects to drive home the piety and resolve of Joseph in the face of adversity:

> The woman in whose house he was solicited him. She locked the doors and said, "Come!" He said, "God forbid! Indeed He is my lord; he has given me a good abode. Indeed the wrongdoers are not felicitous." She made for him; and he would have made for her had he not beheld the proof of his Lord. So it was, that We [God] might turn away from him all evil and indecency. He was indeed one of Our dedicated servants. They raced to the door, and she tore his shirt from behind, and they ran into her husband at the door. She said, "What is to be the requital of him who has evil intentions for your wife except imprisonment or a painful punishment?" (Qur'an 12:23–25)[9]

---

[9] The Qur'anic translations are adapted with slight modifications from 'Al Qul Qar', trans., *The Qur'an: With a Phrase-by-Phrase English Translation* (2005; repr. Elmhurst, NY: Tahrike Tarsile Qur'an Inc., 2011).

A feminist hermeneutic of suspicion, to evoke the language and frameworks developed at length by Elisabeth Schüssler Fiorenza, might ask why the Qur'an's most detailed account of attempted sexual assault involves a woman perpetrator and what this implies for feminist scholarship. From one angle, the story reminds us that it is not sufficient to simply discuss sexual violence in terms of male assaults against females. As a former slave, as a youth, as a victim of familial violence, and as a member of an oppressed social group, at this stage in his life, Joseph (*Yūsuf*) when read through a feminist lens, can represent the intersections of several socially disadvantaged groups that would make him particularly vulnerable to sexual assault and subsequent mistreatment. As to the woman being a perpetrator in this story, she can challenge feminist thought to not simply tokenize women as necessarily on the side of experiencing oppression. Even as the story describes sexual assault, it prompts an examination of the underlying power dynamics that involve but transcend categories of femaleness and maleness.

The power dynamics in the story are particularly evident when Joseph reports the attempted assault against him. When he comes forth, it is he, Joseph, who is punished with imprisonment by the sovereigns. I find this passage critical, as it speaks to a case in which a survivor comes forward alleging sexual assault only to find her/his own integrity cast into doubt. Joseph is blamed and shunned, even in light of the clear physical evidence and testimony that supports his innocence and his efforts to resist and escape: "He [Joseph] said, 'It was she who solicited me.' A witness of her own household testified: 'If his shirt is torn from behind, then she lies and he tells the truth'" (Qur'an 12:26).

In this verse are important communal implications for supporting survivors of violence. First, this verse speaks to the need for any witnesses to give heed to the physical evidence and speak the truth when an alleged assault has occurred. Second, subtle but significant is that someone from the perpetrator's own household comes forward with the testimony. The person gives testimony even though having a kinship relationship to the perpetrator. Another verse of the Qur'an picks up this theme of the necessity to "stand firmly for justice" even against kin or the socially powerful, and especially in cases in which lust could lead one astray:

> O you who believe! Stand out firmly for justice, as witnesses to God, even as against yourselves, or your parents, or your kin, and whether it be one rich or poor: for God has a greater right over them. Follow not lusts, lest you swerve, and if you distort or decline to do justice, verily God is well-acquainted with all that you do. (Qur'an 4:135)

Though taken from another Qur'anic context, this verse seems to have direct bearing on Joseph's situation in the narrative at hand. Despite the physical evidence attesting to the assault upon him, in this narration, the more powerful member of society, in this case the wife of the vizier, receives the light chastisement while the one who was assaulted bears the heavy burden. The situation, in which the corrupt and powerful exploit the disadvantaged, reflects actual social dynamics that feminist thought labors to expose.

Furthermore, the Qur'anic narration makes it clear that the punishment of Joseph was an intentional, not an accidental, oversight of justice: "It occurred to them [the vizier and his advisors], *after they had seen the signs*, to imprison him [Joseph] for a time" (Qur'an 12:35, emphasis added). This verse stresses that those in charge acted punitively toward Joseph, even after having clear indication of what had transpired. The narrative points toward the tendency for corruption in the reporting and prosecuting of sexual assault. It also points toward the impetus to cover potential scandals at the expense of justice. If they seek some type of judicial resolution to the crime of assault, survivors often have to bear such circumstances or even simply the structural lack of capacity of those in positions of power to handle the affair.

Initially, the situation for Joseph is bleak, yet even though he spends a number of years in prison as a result of refusing to cooperate with the advances and schemes of the perpetrator, the narrative still leaves hope that crimes and misconduct can be exposed eventually. Several years later, when pressed, the wife of the vizier finally admits to her culpability in the affair and the truth of the matter is unearthed: "The wife of al-Aziz said: 'Now the truth has become evident. It was I who sought to seduce him, and indeed, he is one of the truthful'" (Qur'an 12:51). This delay in securing some form of justice, even if it amounts to simply an admission of guilt by the perpetrator, is often an excruciating wait for survivors. Lack of truthfulness on the perpetrator's part may also exacerbate the situation. It is no doubt an idealist statement on my part, but perpetrators should readily come forth, despite the consequences and stigmas. From an Islamic theological point of view, justice always prevails, if not in worldly existence, then in an eschatological realm. Although wrongdoing brings consequences, from the Qur'anic perspective, it is ultimately much better to seek forgiveness and make amends while there is still a worldly opportunity to repent, a point to which I will return.

Joseph bore an onerous burden; even though justice was averted for a time, truth does prevail. That justice prevails may not be the experience of survivors, however, each of whom may spend a lifetime waiting on a sense of justice or closure that does not readily materialize. The time between assault and a sense of emotional closure may be lengthy, or it may not come at all, perhaps due to a perpetrator that conceals the wrong, an inadequate justice system, or witnesses that do not come forward. Sometimes, justice may come after trial. One key aspect of the Qur'anic narrative to emphasize here is that the truth prevails in large part because Joseph insists upon extracting it. At opportune moments, he presses his case with those who are in a position of capacity. He leverages what power he does have to elevate and rectify his circumstances. Here, the need for persistent self-advocacy on the part of survivors stands out. Self-advocacy, through reporting a violation and other measures, may not bring healing or closure to an individual survivor, but the act has communal importance that is on the one hand practical and on the other hand metaphysical. On the practical side, reporting and related measures have the potential to prevent further assault by the perpetrator. On the metaphysical side, self-advocacy as an act seeking social justice reifies and elevates the communal standards that protect human dignity. Survivors may find encouragement and courage in Joseph's perseverance and pursuit of justice.

In the Qur'anic narrative, Joseph takes a risk in pressing his case to the sovereign, therein prioritizing his own dignity and reputation, as well as in pursuing the aims of exposing truth and seeking justice. A related question was recently posed to me in a counseling session by a survivor: "Do Muslims have a religious duty to report?" I see reporting and other forms of justice-seeking as meritorious for the reasons immediately above, but I do not find any precedent that would make reporting binding. The question of if a survivor is obligated to report would need more consideration from the standpoint of Islamic legal theory; however, from a moral standpoint, the Qur'an is replete with the commandment to "bid what is right and forbid what is wrong," such as in the following verse: "The faithful men and the faithful women are protectors of one another; they bid what is right and forbid what is wrong" (Qur'an 9:71). Given the possibility that a perpetrator of sexual violence could be a repeat offender, reporting an offense could be seen as part of survivors' responsibilities to "bid what is right" (*ya'murūnabil-ma'rūf*) and "forbid what is wrong" (*yanhūna'anal-munkar*).

Joseph's response to his perpetrator's admission of guilt is also instructive of the moral high road. When the perpetrator confesses to the attempted assault, Joseph offers a definitive reply that is nonetheless full of humility: "Verily God does not guide the deceitful. But nor do I absolve my own self; indeed the self is prone to enjoin evil, except upon those for whom my Lord has mercy. Indeed my lord is forgiving and merciful" (Qur'an 12:52–53). These two verses taken together represent a model for healing. Joseph maintains, on the one hand, a forceful condemnation of immoral and oppressive behavior. Yet, his words acknowledge a core Islamic concept: the self is prone to err and to lose moral control. Joseph's words condemn the assaulter's deceitful behavior while still demonstrating profound compassion. Both orientations, held in a productive tension, seem necessary for trauma healing.

Theodicy, Sexual Violence, and Difficult Texts

The second story of attempted sexual assault in the Qur'an involves a mass of people described as "bewildered in their drunkenness" (Qur'an 15:72) who have intentions to assault the angelic guests visiting the Qur'anic prophets Abraham and Lot. As is typical of Qur'anic narratives, much of the situation must be inferred, and particular details are given in different places in the Qur'an. In one instance, the reproach of Lot to the mob and his plea to his Lord is recounted as follows: "He [Lot] said, 'Indeed I detest your conduct. My Lord! Deliver me and my family from what they do.' So We [God] delivered him and all his family, except an old woman who remained behind" (Qur'an 26:168–72).

As the story unfolds, Lot is instructed by his angelic companions to flee the city, which is subsequently destroyed. The story is a challenging narrative for a feminist lens, both for its implicit condemnation against male same-sex relations and the question of Lot's intentions for offering his daughters in place of his guests, an offer that is understood to be rhetorical and not sincere. Here, however, I want to focus on the plight of Lot and his family away from their home and city in an attempt to escape sexual violence, a scenario that may, unfortunately, resonate with individuals who are facing a similar plight. The savagery of the mob that surrounds Lot's house is suggestive of the horrific manifestations of sexual violence as it occurs in the world, and as such, the Qur'anic story could potentially resonate with those fleeing from sexual exploitation or sexually abusive situations.

In the Qur'anic story, the mob is punished by a powerful rain, and the might and mercy of God are emphasized: "Then We [God] destroyed the others, and rained down upon them a rain. Evil was the rain [upon] those who were warned! There is indeed a sign in that; but most of them do not have faith. Indeed your Lord is the Allmighty, the All-merciful"(Qur'an 172-75).

Although the story may give hope for God's justice to those who have narrowly escaped sexual assault, the story might not resonate at all with survivors who did not have the privilege of being whisked away from harm in the company of angelic beings in an immediate answer to their supplications as were Lot and (most of) his family. The story certainly gives rise to questions of theodicy, even as the narrative centers on God's justice and the triumph of the faithful. Regarding perpetrators of violence, this story assures that their deceitful intents will be recompensed, sooner or later.

The Qur'an is replete with verses that condemn wrongdoing and promise punishment, yet at the same time, a host of Qur'anic verses suggest the possibility of God's forgiveness and mercy in cases of earnest repentance and accountability, such as the following:

> And those who, when they commit an indecent act (*fāḥishah*), or wrong themselves, remember God, and plead forgiveness for their sins—and who forgives sins except God?—*and who do not persist in what they have committed while they know*. Their reward is forgiveness from their Lord, and gardens with streams running in them, in which to forever remain. How excellent is the reward of the workers! (Qur'an 3:135-36, emphasis added)

From a survivor's perspective, this passage may seem to readily excuse a potential perpetrator of sexual violence; however, the verses above also are preceded by additional required virtues, such as refraining from usury, spending generously of wealth in ease and adversity, suppressing anger, and excusing faults of others. Appropriate emphasis should be put on the last clause of verse 3:135, which states clearly that persistence in wrongdoing while knowing the morally correct course of action is inexcusable. In the Qur'an, forgiveness for sexual misconduct may be possible, but sincerity in the process of seeking forgiveness (known in Arabic as *istaghfār*) requires a profound sincerity and resolve to never return to the moral wrong. For survivors of violence, the prayer of Lot in verse 26:168 mentioned above, alongside God's immediate response, stresses the potency of earnest supplication and the possibility of God responding to faithful prayers. The promise that God hears and responds to supplication is central to Qur'anic discourse, present in verses such as "Your Lord has said, 'Call Me, and I will hear you!" (Qur'an 40:60).

Likewise, the divine epithet All-Hearing (*al-samīʿ*) alone appears in 45 or more places throughout the Qur'an. For those seeking spiritual healing from within a theistic faith framework, divine appellations such as this one may bring comfort and spiritual healing. Other Qur'anic axioms of encouragement for survivors include the promise of God's ultimate justice and the description of the resilience given to individual souls: "God tasks no soul beyond its capacity. It shall have what it has earned and be subject to what it has perpetrated" (Qur'an 2:286) and "No soul does evil except against itself, and no bearer shall bear another's burden; then to your Lord will be your return, whereat He will inform you concerning that about which you used to differ" (Qur'an 6:164). The idea that God "tasks no soul beyond its capacity" does not mean that people will not be tested at all. In fact, when describing life's moments of adversity, the Qur'an regularly reminds that the entire purpose of life for human beings is to be tested (e.g., Qur'an 6:165). When trials, such as overcoming sexual violence or struggling against abuse, come to a person, from an Islamic perspective, the circumstances should be met with strength and resolve, not passivity or hopelessness. Strength and resolve are maintained by turning attention and supplication to strengthening the soul, through a connection to the One who dispenses ultimate justice.

Qur'anic Prohibitions against Sexual Assault

It is abundantly clear that much of what is termed sexual assault in the contemporary age is also abhorrent from the Qur'anic worldview; sexual assault is a crime against both God and fellow humans. The Qur'an explicitly forbids illicit sexual relations and gives some instruction on how to deal with claims of sexual misconduct.[10] The perpetrators of imprudent acts are repeatedly condemned in the Qur'an with clear prohibitions such as the following: "Do not approach illicit sexual relations (*zinā*). It is indeed an indecency (*fāḥishah*) and an evil way" (Qur'an 17:32). Individuals are regularly commanded to guard themselves against impermissible sexual acts, described literally as "preserving the orifices" (*ḥifẓ al-furūj*). This command to sexual decency is mentioned in the Qur'an in several places alongside the commandments to keep mindful prayers, guard against idle talk, and keep oaths (e.g., Qur'an 23:1–10), all of which are central religious obligations.[11]

---

[10] I am treating this subject in a forthcoming work, as it requires a longer discussion than is possible here.

[11] What precisely constitutes *fāḥishah* is up for hermeneutical dispute, including among queer Muslim theologians. Furthermore, the line between reciprocal sex and forced sex is an issue that presents difficulty in carrying out justice for the victim in the wake of sexual assault. Questions regarding the role of consent are highly pertinent. Generally, scholars who set the foundations of Islamic law emphasized consent at the moment a marriage contract was agreed upon, but consent for each instance of conjugal relations was historically not emphasized. These are all matters that require a much more detailed treatment than is possible here. For a detailed treatment of marriage, concubinage, and sexual ethics, see Kecia Ali, *Marriage and Slavery in Early Islam* (Cambridge, MA: Harvard University Press, 2010). See also Kecia Ali, "Obedience and Disobedience in Islamic Discourses," *Encyclopedia of Women in Islamic Cultures*, ed. Suad Joseph (Leiden, Netherlands: Brill, 2007), 309–13.

Opposing Sexual Assault while Simultaneously Resisting Other Forms of Violence

Responsible feminist scholarship cannot be myopic. I am keenly aware that when I explore sexual violence and gender tropes in the Qur'an, I do so from a vantage point within the United States, where anti-Islamic sentiment is virulent, Muslims are among the least warmly received groups,[12] Muslim men are understood to be uniquely inclined to commit acts of insolence and physical violence upon women and girls, and where Muslim women and girls are perceived to be uniquely or particularly vulnerable because of their religious or cultural background.[13] Cultural anthropologist Lila Abu-Lughod has analyzed at length how the trope of "defending the rights of Muslim women was offered as part of the justification for U.S. military intervention in Afghanistan."[14] More recently, Rania Khalek pointed to the resurfacing of this dynamic as a similar interventionist trope is used with respect to women in ISIS-occupied territory.[15] Khalek describes a double standard in mainstream American news cycles, wherein acts of violence perpetrated by Americans or American allies receive little attention, compared to acts of violence committed by anti-American actors. In one example, Ambassador-at-Large for Global Women's Issues Catherine Russel laments the "young girls, mothers, and sisters

---

[12] For study details, see "How Americans Feel about Religious Groups: Jews, Catholics, and Evangelicals Rated Warmly, Atheists and Muslims More Coldly," *Pew Research Center*, July 16, 2014, http://www.pewforum. org/files/2014/07/Views-of-Religious-Groups-09-22-final.pdf.

[13] For a discussion around the positioning of Muslim girls as sites of violence especially within discourses of child marriage, see Shenila Khoja-Moolji, "Girls, Education, and Narratives of Progress: Deconstructing the Discourse on Child Marriage," in *Educating Adolescent Girls around the Globe: Challenges and Implications*, ed. Sandra Stacki and Supriya Baily (New York: Routledge, 2015).

[14] Lila Abu-Lughod, *Do Muslim Women Need Saving?* (Cambridge, MA: Harvard University Press, 2013), 4. See esp. "Authorizing Moral Crusades," 82–112. For a discussion around the positioning of Muslim girls as sites of violence, see Khoja-Moolji, "Girls, Education, and Narratives of Progress."

[15] Rania Khalek, "Drone Strike Feminism Using the Oppression of Women to Sell Another Iraq War," *FAIR*, November 1, 2014, http://fair.org/extra-online-articles/drone-strike-feminism/.

facing imminent rape, trafficking, and forced marriage" who "pleaded to be killed in airstrikes rather than be brutalized by ISIL."[16] Russel's remark, particularly given her diplomatic position, can be interpreted as legitimating state-sponsored violence as the better option to gender-based violence. Little attention is given to the structural conditions, discourses, and geopolitics that place vulnerable people in situations in which *both* state-sponsored violence and gender-based violence are imminent threats and excruciating realities.

I share Russel's empathy for the unspeakable violence endured by women and girls living in or fleeing from war zones. Russel's opinion piece focuses on concubinage, violence against women, and women's forced conversion to Islam. These are ultimately inseparable from the violence that also affects men and boys, who are dehumanized, subjected to traumas of war and displacement, and subjected to physical violence and shaming, all of which are exacerbated by militarization and arms proliferation. In short, crimes of sexual violence are tied up in geopolitical webs that make moving beyond the unhelpful politicization of the issue difficult. One such problematic approach for addressing sexual suffering is that of Ayan Hirsi Ali, whose namesake foundation was set up in 2007 to, according to the foundation's website, "help protect and defend the rights of women in the U.S. from religiously and culturally instigated oppression."[17] I cite this initiative here as an instance of anti-sexual-violence advocacy that may be well-meaning but feeds into the larger trend of singling out Muslims, and immigrants in particular, as perpetrators of sexual abuse and violence. For instance, one foundation publication is

---

[16] Catherine Russel, "ISIL's Abuse of Women and Girls Must Be Stopped," *World Post*, September 12, 2014, http://www.huffingtonpost.com/catherine-russell/isils-abuse-of-women-and-_b_5807226.html.

[17] The Ayan Hirsi Ali Foundation focuses on "honor violence," "forced marriage," and "female genital mutilation" and conducts "lobbying and outreach to expand and strengthen state and national legislation for the protection of women and girls." It provides trainings for law-enforcement public-service providers and published a national resource directory of shelters and legal aid organizations. See AHA Foundation, "About," accessed January 10, 2015, http://theahafoundation.org/about/.

intended to inform "U.S. educators, social workers and law enforcement personnel" about how they "ought not to contribute—passively or actively—to the oppression of women within 'other' cultures."[18]

This binary between service providers as representing one discrete culture and Muslims representing another discrete culture is a recurring feature of the publication. The publication also sets up Muslims in the United States as either "moderate" or "fundamentalist" and is replete with language that pits good "moderates" again bad "fundamentalists." Such binary caricatures fail to capture the nuance and range of values and attitudes within the American Muslim community on issues pertaining to religion, sexual ethics, and family life. The caricatures of Muslims depicted in the publication can be highly demeaning to those Muslims who consider fundamentals of Islamic religious practice important in their lives and who also abhor sexual violence. With its lens trained on the plight of Muslim women and girls, the publication overlooks the widespread struggles against sexual violence in the broader American context. Focusing almost exclusively on sensational vignettes involving young immigrant girls, rather than on thoroughly researched sociological studies about trends in sexual violence in the United States, the publication gives the impression that if a self-identified Muslim or a person with ties to a majority-Muslim country is involved in an act of sexual violence, that act was "committed in the name of Islam."[19] Religion is depicted as the grounds upon which abuse is legitimated, without sufficient evidence. After detailing several horrendous abuse cases—most pertaining to children of Muslim immigrants in predominantly Christian societies—the publication depicts the pressing

---

[18] AHA Foundation, "What Do We Know? Facts and Figures on the Circumstances Affecting Muslim Girls and Women in the United States," December 18, 2009, 13, http://theahafoundation.org/wp/wp-content/uploads/2011/05/AHA-2009-What-Do-We-Know-1.pdf.

[19] Ibid., 2. The extent to which self-identified Muslims, compared to persons of other confessional religious groups or cultural identities, are involved in incidents of sexual violence is not clear; nor is the extent to which religion specifically is a factor.

need to rescue helpless girls.[20] Even more remarkably, the publication's arguments are framed by citations to the works of prominent Muslim feminist scholars taken out of context.[21]

As Ayesha Chaudhry details at length, Muslim feminist engagement must navigate xenophobia, Islamophobia, and anti-Muslim bias, even as Muslim feminists attempt to address sociopolitical issues related to gender. To be explicit, sexual violence and abuse is a pressing matter, but it is not a uniquely a Muslim phenomenon or an issue of immigrant assimilation. To the contrary, as I am repeatedly reminded in my own interactions with service providers in college and university campus settings in particular, sexual violence is not confined to particular cultural or religious affiliations. In my interactions with assault survivors, only some of them Muslim, I am struck by their resiliency and reminded of the approach of Abu-Lughod, who brings to the forefront nuanced depictions of women coping with life challenges and struggles with dignity, courage, and hope. She explicitly invites readers to note and appreciate the resilience and creativity of her informants through lenses other than the historically dominant ones of colonial feminism and Christian mission.[22]

---

[20] For a provocative account of the attention paid to young Muslim girls and what it conceals, see Shenila Khoja-Moolji, "Suturing together Girls and Education: An Investigation into the Social (Re)Production of Girls' Education as a Hegemonic Ideology," *Journal of Diaspora, Indigenous, and Minority Education*, 9, no. 2 (2015): 87–107.

[21] For a provocative discussion of this tension, see Jasmine Zine, "Between Orientalism and Fundamentalism: The Politics of Muslim Women's Feminist Engagement," *Muslim World Journal of Human Rights* 3, no. 1 (2006): 1–24.

[22] In light of the historical dominance of such hegemonic discourses, Muslim-led grassroots interventions and mobilizations may help to provide safe space. For instance, a Chicago-based organization, HEART Women and Girls, produces and disseminates reproductive-health education and healthy relationship literature geared to different Muslim contexts. The organization runs an anonymous question-and-answer forum and trains peer volunteers who are equipped to serve at the communal level. Their work is multifaceted and entails being present for individuals recovering from sexual violations, spiritually supporting individuals who are ostracized by the larger community for identifying as gay or queer, and providing resources for individuals struggling with a religiously grounded emphasis on abstinence outside of marriage.

Scholarship as Feminist Resistance, Lingering Questions

As the essays in this volume detail, sexual assault occurs in many different contexts. It is an instrument of warfare; it is present in the daily traumas endured by sex workers, in the abuse of the young, and in various other misappropriations of power or force. It is present in cases of intimate partner abuse, in the context of unwanted advances, and in circumstances when a person's judgment is impaired. Political instabilities, economic insecurity, and horrendous oppression and injustice have brought about such dire humanitarian crises in a handful of regions that ruminating about sexual violence from a place of privilege within the academy seems an almost frivolous enterprise. At the same time, this lived reality takes me back to central questions and tensions in this endeavor: What, exactly, makes sexual violence a particularly worthy site of concern when violence in general is rampant and sexual violence is just one of its many forms?[23] To my own context, can *Muslima* theology play a role in responding to—or even ameliorating—sexual violence within *and beyond* Muslim contexts? And to our shared context, how likely is it that feminist ruminations and novel scriptural hermeneutics will have positive impacts on behalf of those affected by sexual violence? As this volume shows, to think and to write, as occupations of their own, are important as means of "restoring agency" and "enabling healing,"[24] as ways of being "educated and empowered by our interactions with sacred texts,"[25] and as paths toward reclaiming our integrity as wo/men and as religious feminists.

---

[23] For one provocative exploration of this question, see Valerie M. Hudson, Bonnie Ballif-Spanvill, Mary Caprioli, and Chad F. Emmett, *Sex and World Peace* (New York: Columbia University Press, 2012).
[24] See the arguments of Amy Kalmanofsky ("How Feminist Biblical Scholarship Can Heal Victims of Sexual Violation," chapter 1).
[25] Sarra Lev, "'Dipping a Finger in Honey,'" chapter 3.

CHAPTER 5

Naming Violence: Qur'anic Interpretation between Social Justice and Cultural Relativism
Ayesha S. Chaudhry

"Religious feminists" are central figures in the kind of work that this volume seeks to address; that is, they seek "to identify methods of interpretation that could engender a process of healing from sexual violence and abuse perpetrated in and through sacred scripture." In their attempt to engage in such work, however, they often come under vehement critique from various parties. It turns out, then, that religious feminists occupy a difficult, if not an impossible, space. The very term *religious feminist* is seen by some as an oxymoron. *Patriarchal coreligionists*, who promote patriarchal versions of the religion; *cultural relativist liberals*, who suspend all moral judgment when approaching a culture they do not consider their own;[1] and *supercessionist feminists*, who see religion as irredeemably patriarchal, all accuse religious feminists of "inauthenticity" and of "compromising" fundamental values of religion and feminism, respectively. Throughout this essay, I will use the terms *patriarchal Muslims, cultural relativist liberals,* and *supercessionist feminists* for ease and accuracy of reference.

---

[1] Cultural relativist liberals can be Muslims, as well as people outside of the Muslim community, who engage in similar reasoning about Islam and Muslims elsewhere.

On the one hand, supercessionist feminists accuse religious feminists of not being liberal or feminist enough because they are unwilling to give up their religious identity in favor of liberalism and/or feminism. These liberals wonder why religious feminists opt to remain part of religious traditions that are fundamentally and essentially patriarchal and illiberal and that cannot be extricated from their patriarchal roots. Why remain part of a tradition that creates and institutionalizes discriminatory gender binaries, privileging men and disempowering women? Why not give up this religious identity altogether and get to the "real" work of improving women's rights and fighting for social justice and democracy? Why remain part of a religious tradition wherein still, in 2016, the equal human worth of men and women is a contested, hotly debated, and even an inflammatory topic?[2]

On the other hand, patriarchal coreligionists accuse religious feminists of not being religious enough because they are unwilling to give up their feminists beliefs in favor of religious submission. They wonder why religious feminists impose a perceived extra-religious, non-divine feminist discourse on their religious traditions and why those feminists question, if not undermine, some of the most basic presuppositions upon which the tradition and religious authority are built. Why privilege a feminist tradition that seems to hate men and constantly disrespects religious authorities? Why not give up this feminist identity altogether and get to the "real" work of improving human dignity and fighting for social justice? Why stick to a fight that is really "not that important" or central, and

---

[2] The field of religious feminism is rich and vibrant. For a sample of sources of Jewish, Christian, and Muslim feminisms, see Riv-Ellen Prell, ed., *Women Remaking American Judaism* (Detroit, MI: Wayne State University Press, 2007); Serene Jones, *Feminist Theory and Christian Theology: Cartographies of Grace* (Minneapolis, MN: Augsburg Fortress, 2000); Phyllis Trible, *Texts of Terror: Literary-Feminist Readings of Biblical Narratives* (Minneapolis, MN: Fortress, 1984); and Ziba Mir-Hosseini, "Beyond 'Islam' vs. 'Feminism,'" *Institute of Development Studies Bulletin* 42, no. 1 (2011): 67–77. For activist scholarship in Islamic feminisms, see Musuwah, For Equality in the Muslim Family, http://www.musawah.org.

instead focus on social-justice projects that actually make the world a better place, like ending war, alleviating poverty, or increasing access to water?

Usually, these critiques of religious feminists, from all sides, betray an assumption that both feminism and religion are essentialist, undifferentiated, and uncontested discourses, in which all difference is subsumed under one or a few umbrella concepts or beliefs. And because the categories of feminism and religion are fundamentally heterogeneous—there are many kinds of feminisms and ways to express faith in every religious tradition—it should come as no surprise that religious feminisms also appear in multiple forms. Some are more or less accommodating of patriarchal religious traditions and/or feminist ideals.[3]

In this essay, I reflect on the impossible space occupied by religious feminists, in particular Muslim feminists, through the lens of my own experiences in this field. I recently published a book entitled *Domestic Violence and the Islamic Tradition: Ethics, Law and the Muslim Discourse on Gender*.[4] This book is devoted to the study of a particular Qur'anic verse (4:34), which has historically been interpreted as prescribing, not just permitting, husbands to hit their wives as a disciplinary measure. The book examines the intellectual history of Muslim discussions on this topic from the ninth century to the twenty-first century through a study of Qur'an commentaries and legal discussions. Here I share these arguments in summary form.

My research demonstrates that the precolonial Islamic tradition, as captured in the textual traditions of Qur'an commentaries and Islamic law, is uniformly, unashamedly, and unsurprisingly patriarchal. As such, the precolonial Islamic tradition assumed that the right

---

[3] Amy Kalmanofsky's paper in this volume raises the important question about who religious feminists seek to heal, who they seek to save: victims of violence, God, scripture, or religious traditions ("How Feminist Biblical Scholarship Can Heal Victims of Sexual Violation," chapter 1).

[4] Ayesha S. Chaudhry, *Violence and the Islamic Tradition: Ethics, Law, and the Muslim Discourse on Gender* (Oxford: Oxford University Press, 2014).

of husbands to discipline their wives through various measures, including physical violence, was a fundamental marital privilege. Not a single scholar questioned this right; the ethical discourse about domestic violence was about procedure rather than the fact of this right. Conversations were always about *how* and *when* husbands should physically discipline their wives, rather than *if* they should.

Postcolonial Muslim scholarly and activist discourse about Qur'an 4:34 has shifted, so that the right of husbands to hit their wives has become contested on moral grounds. This means that in the postcolonial period, discussion of the topic—for the first time in Muslim history—includes questions of gender justice. Centrally, the idea that husbands may hit their wives for any reason, whether for disciplinary purposes or not, no longer conforms with Muslim views about justice, gender, or a good God. Given that reality, Muslims are now asking why God would interrupt human history to re-instantiate a patriarchal ordering of the genders and, in a context wherein women are already disempowered, command that husbands hit their wives when they are disobedient. Because this dispensation does not accord with modern ideas about a just God, Muslim scholars have offered new, nonviolent, interpretations of the Qur'anic text so that, when faced with marital discord, Muslims are encouraged to separate rather than be violent.[5]

I ask why some Muslim scholars still feel compelled to follow precolonial patriarchal and violent readings of Qur'an 4:34 when they can choose to follow any of the postcolonial nonviolent interpretations. This question is not simply theoretical or rhetorical, nor is it merely academic; rather, it has real implications for women today.

---

[5] Hundreds of millions of Muslims today believe in a gender-equal Islam and see no contradiction between "Western" values and "Islam." See Celene Ibrahim's paper in this volume, in which she argues that contemporary notions of "sexual assault" were also "abhorrent in the Qur'anic worldview," even though classical Islamic jurists did not see unwanted sex as necessarily constitutive of sexual assault ("Sexual Violence and Qur'anic Resources for Healing Processes," chapter 4).

Many Muslim-majority countries, such as the United Arab Emirates, have legalized domestic violence by citing violent interpretations of Qur'an 4:34. Indeed, the personal status and penal codes of several Muslim-majority countries protect the right of husbands to physically discipline their wives through explicit reference to Qur'an 4:34.[6]

Based on discussions of what I call idealized cosmologies and the egalitarian-authoritative dilemma, I argue that scholars and communities have powerful agency when determining which Qur'anic interpretations they choose to follow. I urge Muslims to shift authority away from a precolonial patriarchal religious tradition toward the living Muslim community; I urge Muslim communities to choose interpretations that protect living, unnamed women rather than protect a tradition of dead, named men.[7]

Though my presentations examine the distinct characteristics of pre- and postcolonial Muslim engagement with the issue of domestic violence, I consistently encounter two particular criticisms that have to do more with my positionality than my research. First, cultural relativist liberal interlocutors question whether using the term *domestic violence* to describe the physical discipline of wives is anachronistic. These interlocutors prefer that I use the term *light tapping* or *discipline*, and avoid the terms *wife beating* and *domestic violence*, because these terms somehow have the dual effect of misrepresenting the main message of the Qur'an *and* making Muslims look bad to others, confirming the views of those who consider Islam to be a misogynistic religion. These critics, even when they understand the Arabic phrase "*wa-ḍribūhunna*" in Qur'an 4:34 to mean "hit/beat/strike them," prefer that I refer to this as a *light* or *gentle tapping*. Second, based on my criticism

---

[6] Ayesha S. Chaudhry, "Interrogating the 'Shari'a' Excuse: Religious Reasoning, International Law and the Struggle for Gender Equality in the Middle East," in *The Evolving Roles of Women in the Arab World: Empowering Women after the Arab Spring*, ed. Marwa Shalaby and Valentine M. Moghadam (New York: Palgrave Macmillan, 2016).
[7] Ayesha S. Chaudhry, *Domestic Violence and the Islamic Tradition: Ethics, Law, and the Muslim Discourse on Gender* (New York: Oxford University Press, 2013).

of Muslim scholars who refuse to abandon violent interpretations of Qur'an 4:34 in favor of nonviolent interpretations offered by modern Muslim scholars, both patriarchal Muslims and cultural relativist liberals ask me why or how I feel comfortable importing "Western" and/or "modern" views about gender equality into "Islam." In doing so, am I not imposing a "Western hegemony" on "Islam and Muslims" and forcing them to acquiesce to "Western" standards of justice?

Let me unpack the second critique that posits an easy separation between Islam and the West, and then work my way back to thinking about the first criticism of using the term *domestic violence* to describe the act of husbands hitting their wives as an act of divinely sanctioned marital discipline. Though I have faced the critique of importing Western values into Islam from cultural relativist liberals and patriarchal Muslims alike, these critiques result from separate lines of reasoning and serve varying purposes. Let us examine this critique first from a patriarchal Muslim perspective and then from a feminist and liberal perspective.

Saving Islam at the Expense of Muslim Women

When patriarchal Muslims criticize Muslim feminists for importing Western values into Islam, they posit both the West and Islam as static, discrete, self-contained, and opposing entities. In this conception, the West is characterized as a political enemy of Islam, through reference to colonialism and neo-imperialism. It is also described as a place of social and sexual anarchy, moral chaos, depraved values, and the destruction of the family. Thus, in light of the presumed political animosity and moral failings of the West, accusing someone of adopting Western standards of justice is to accuse that person of being an "orientalist" who is trying to "corrupt and destroy Islam."[8] In this

---

[8] All phrases in quotations are actual criticisms I have received.

framework, feminism is conceived of as a "Western project," and as such, it conjures up all the negative connotations associated with colonialism and imperialism. In contrast, Islam is represented as a pristine, pure, divine faith that must be protected from the onslaught of the West, which seeks to destroy core values of Islam. This pristine Islam is best preserved in the precolonial Islamic tradition, before Muslims became corrupted through Western influences.

To be fair, this oppositional narrative of Islam and the West emerged from the disingenuous alliance between feminist discourse and the colonialist project. It is well documented that both Christian and feminist rhetoric were used to justify the colonialist project. Though colonialism may be a distant memory for many Westerners, it is a living and very recent memory for hundreds of millions of Muslims who struggled under colonialism and fought for independence from foreign colonialist invasions as recently as five decades ago and who are still suffering in its wake in the postcolonial period. This means that the colonial experience is still a living memory for Muslims, which accounts for the power wielded by anti-feminist rhetoric by associating feminism with colonialism and imperialism.[9]

Given the highly politicized nature of women's rights in the postcolonial context, patriarchal Muslims have taken to interpreting Islamic law/sharia (terms that they use interchangeably) in a patriarchal manner, denying Muslim women equal rights in the public and private spheres. This patriarchal interpretation of Islamic law relies on patriarchal elements of the precolonial Islamic scholarship to express authenticity. Though those who champion a patriarchal interpretation of Islamic law cling to the patriarchy of precolonial Islamic scholarship, they are willing to institute reforms in other areas of Islamic law, such as creating financial instruments for use within the global economy, adopting modern technologies wholesale, and abolishing slavery.[10]

---

[9] See the works of Leila Ahmed and Ziba Mir-Hosseini, among others.
[10] For example, the Gulf countries and Saudi Arabia.

For patriarchal Muslims who see Islam and the West as oppositional, feminism is Western and therefore un-Islamic, and Islam is best captured in precolonial Islamic scholarship, particularly in its patriarchal manifestations. According to patriarchal Muslims, because the precolonial Islamic tradition was thoroughly patriarchal, the patriarchy of Islamic scholarship accurately reflects how God created humans, with essentially gendered characteristics. Patriarchy, in this conception, does not denigrate men or women; rather, it values their natures as they were created and thereby frees them to be "real and full" men and women. In this view, feminism is a "pernicious," "dangerous," and "evil" force that seeks to corrupt Muslims by introducing the idea that women and men are equal, not just spiritually but also socially.[11] Muslim feminist thought is seen as a Trojan horse, and Muslim feminists, male and female, represent a great danger to Muslims from within, threatening to destroy the unity of Muslims. In this light, the idea of Muslim feminists or Islamic feminism is an oxymoron; any "Western" expression of Islam, especially a "feminist" Islam, is seen as inauthentic. Such an Islam privileges "Western" values of gender equality over "Islamic" values of patriarchy, and it exalts human reason and contemporary mores over and above a divine system that true believers submit to uncritically. By promoting feminist ideas, Muslim feminists demonstrate, at best, their "weak" and "compromised" faith and, at worst, their lack of faith and commitment to Islam.

The metaphor of the Trojan horse is apt here, because Islamic feminism is deeply threatening to the brand of patriarchal Islam that posits Islam and feminism as mutually exclusive categories. In fact, it is so threatening that patriarchal Muslims are willing to declare Muslim feminists apostates and/or infidels: people who have renounced

---

[11] These are precisely the words used by patriarchal Muslims to describe feminism. For example, see Amad Sheikh, "Abu Eesa (AE): Humor Overload, Feminism and Apologies," March 11, 2014, http://muslimmatters.org/2014/03/11/abu-eesa-humor-overload-and-apologies/.

Islam and are representatives of external agendas that seek to destroy Islam. The faith claims of Muslim feminists are deemed disingenuous and misleading. Because religious feminists, in this case Muslim feminists, are deeply invested in their religious identities and seek to reform Muslim communities to become more gender equal from within the Islamic framework, charges of apostasy and heresy are painful, invalidating the very foundation on which the Muslim feminists stand. Charges of apostasy and heresy carry physical dangers. In addition to challenging the authority and sincerity of Muslim feminists, such charges make one liable to criminal prosecution in fifteen Muslim-majority countries and carry the death penalty in nine.

Further, in a world where the radicalism of Da'esh (aka, ISIS) is appealing to at least some Muslims living in minority contexts, charges of apostasy, or even questioning the faith of Muslim feminists, is irresponsible in posing a danger to the accused, and yet, Muslims who champion patriarchal visions of Islam are more likely to challenge the faith of Muslim feminists than they are the faith of groups such as Da'esh.[12] For example, Yasir Qadhi (also spelled "Kazi"), assistant professor at Rhodes College and dean of Academic Affairs at Al-Maghrib Institute (an online forum for Islamic education), is more comfortable declaring Muslim feminists apostates than he is declaring Da'esh such. He writes about the attempt of Muslim feminists to reform gender-discriminatory laws such as the laws of inheritance, which grant sons twice the inheritance of daughters:

> I would be unwilling to call for reform in, say, the Islamic laws of inheritance, since these have been explicitly laid out in the Sacred Texts. If some people consider rejecting the explicit texts of the Qur'an to be "Islamic feminism," then I

---

[12] For a wonderfully sophisticated and accessible exploration of the "Islamic" nature of Da'esh, see Anver Emon, "Is ISIS Islamic? Why It Matters for the Study of Islam," March 27, 2015, http://blogs.ssrc.org/tif/2015/03/27/is-isis-islamic-why-it-matters-for-the-study-of-islam/.

> view it as being a manifestation of *kufr* [infidelity],[13] and you count me an ardent opponent of any such endeavor. Anyone who wishes to supplant the Sacred Texts with another ideology does so because of a simultaneous lack of faith in the Divine Revelation of Allah, and an inferiority complex to another system of laws and culture.[14]

Notice how Qadhi is entirely dismissive of the gender-equal interpretations of the laws of inheritance offered by Muslim feminists and speaks for God when claiming access to the "true" meaning of the Qur'an. Rather than even consider the content of Muslim feminist interpretations or treat them as an alternative point of view with which he might respectfully disagree, Qadhi rejects attempts at such interpretations as a "manifestation of infidelity." Note also the oppositional relationship posited between feminism and Islam such that Muslim feminists are infidels, lacking faith and suffering from an inferiority complex. They are not sincere believers struggling to remain a part of the Muslim faith community while maintaining their integrity and dignity as human beings, regardless of their gender. In contrast to his harsh judgment of Islamic feminism, Qadhi is open to assuming the religious sincerity of Da'esh members, about whom he writes: "I have called ISIS 'neo-Kharijites,' and have criticized some of their tactics. I have and am always willing to defend my position. (For the record, I do not accuse them of *kufr* [infidelity] or *nifaq* [hyprocrisy]—I might disagree with their tactics and worldview, but I don't expel them from the fold of Islam)."[15]

---

[13] Note that a *kāfir* is an "infidel" and can be one who was never Muslim but when a Muslim is accused of committing *kufr* (infidelity) or of becoming a *kāfir* (infidel), this a charge of apostasy. The act of saying that a Muslim is committing infidelity or has become an infidel is *takfir*, and this is precisely what Qadhi is doing here; he is doing the *takfir* of Muslim feminists. The punishment for apostasy in classical Islamic law is death.

[14] Yasir Qadhi, "Thoughts on (AE) Abu Eesa-Gate," Muslim Matters, March 14, 2014: http://muslimmatters.org/2014/03/14/yasir-qadhi-thoughts-on-abu-eesa-gate/.

[15] This quotation is taken from Qadhi's public Facebook page, accessed September 21, 2015, https://www.facebook.com/yasir.qadhi/posts/10152948567153300.

According to Qadhi, there is no constructive way to engage with Islamic feminists because their commitment to gender equality is so antithetical to the patriarchal nature of Islam as to push them outside the pale of Islam itself. In contrast, though Qadhi is interested in opposing Da'esh, he sees himself as having enough common ground with them in terms of beliefs that he feels that charging them with infidelity or even hypocrisy is neither useful nor appropriate. For Qadhi, he and Da'esh simply disagree in their interpretations of sacred texts, but Muslim feminists reject the sacred text altogether, rather than offering alternative readings of the text. Because Qadhi sees Islam as fundamentally patriarchal and gender equality as a fundamentally Western value, for him, a gender-equal reading of Islam necessarily imposes Western values on Islam and thereby represents domination of Islam.[16]

Positing an inherent opposition between Islam and the West—and, by extension, feminism—is a deeply contradictory and sanctimonious move for patriarchal Muslims such as Qadhi, who live as Muslims in the Western world and are both Muslim and Western. Patriarchal Muslims arbitrarily deem some values and expressions of the "West" as Islamic while rejecting others as un-Islamic. It is difficult to see these judgments as principled rather than opportunistic. For example, patriarchal Muslims have relied on their individual and communal rights as citizens and minorities in democratic nation-states to lobby for sharia courts in the United Kingdom (successfully) and Canada (unsuccessfully) to oversee the application of a gender-discriminatory Islamic family law. These same advocates have

---

[16] Ironically, even though Qadhi believes that he has more of a common ground for a constructive conversation with Da'esh, he has been declared a *murtadd* (apostate) by them as a result of his denunciation of the Charlie Hebdo murders. That Qadhi is more willing to charge Muslim feminists with apostasy rather than Da'esh, a group that has now charged him with apostasy, demonstrates how threatening Islamic feminism is for his brand of patriarchal Islam. See "From Hypocrisy to Apostasy: The Extinction of the Grayzone," *Dabiq* 7 (2015): 54–66, http://media.clarionproject.org/files/islamic-state/islamic-state-dabiq-magazine-issue-7-from-hypocrisy-to-apostasy.pdf.

critiqued Muslim feminists, including myself, as importing otherwise alien Western values of individual rights and human rights into Islam when we argue for interpreting Islamic law to be gender equal; however, they do not see themselves as importing Western values into Islamic discourse when they use the language of individual and human rights to petition for sharia courts.

The drama of protecting a patriarchal Islam against a gender-egalitarian Islam also plays out on the global stage, wherein those who are not Muslim are drawn into this debate and forced to pick a side by making a claim about whose representation of Islam is most "authentic" and "true." This can be seen, for example, in the reservations that many Muslim-majority states have expressed to Article 16 of the Convention on the Elimination of All Forms of Discrimination against Women. Article 16 seeks to improve women's rights in family law by giving them equal rights when entering a marriage, reciprocal rights for the duration of the marriage, and equal rights when exiting the marriage. Most of the countries that expressed reservations to Article 16 are Muslim-majority countries, and the majority of those countries cited Islamic law or sharia as the reason for their reservation. Affording women equal rights in family law, they argue, is antithetical to their commitment to Islamic law, so the global community ought to respect their religious tradition to discriminate against women in family law.[17] In making this argument, these countries are pitting liberal values against each other—that is, religious tolerance and pluralism against gender equality. These nation-states want to alter the narrative of women's rights so that instead of being a discussion about protecting women against discrimination, the conversation is transformed to focus on protecting the national sovereignty and religious integrity of Muslim-majority nation-states against Western imperialist influences.

---

[17] Chaudhry, "Interrogating the 'Shari'a' Excuse."

This characterization of Islam and the West is inherently essentialist and ignores the complexity and diversity of both these terms. It also rejects and ignores the globalized nature of the contemporary world and the fact that the West and Islam are not even overlapping categories. One is a geographic region and the other is a religion. The very fact that I often encounter the criticism of imposing Western values on Islam after I deliver a paper in the English language in a Western country indicates that the very participants in this conversation—including myself—embody and perform multiple identities, including "Islamic" and "Western," at once. While many of these same Muslims criticize the media for ignoring the wildly differing expressions of Islam and Muslims around the world, painting Islam in broad strokes, they themselves describe Islam as a uniform religion and reject any expression of feminist Islam as inauthentic and as not emerging from within the Islamic tradition. Patriarchal Muslims such as Qadhi seek to protect the patriarchy of the Islamic tradition from "feminist" assault, even if that means protecting an interpretation that preserves a patriarchal reading of Qur'an 4:34 that disempowers women and sanctions violence against them. Their concern for the tradition and for traditionalist scholars trumps their concern for the well-being of Muslim women who stand to be discriminated against and harmed from violent interpretations of this verse.

Who "Owns" Gender Equality?

Muslims who champion a patriarchal Islam are not alone in positing the oppositional narrative between the West and Islam. Cultural relativist liberals—whether from within or without the Muslim community—also pitch the West and Islam as mutually exclusive categories. When cultural relativist liberals critique my advocacy of a gender-egalitarian Islamic law and theology, they ask me why I am imposing Western values on Islam and whether I worry about imposing a hegemonic imperialist framework on Islam. Their question makes truth claims about the nature of the West and Islam as static, discrete, self-contained, and opposing entities; the West is characterized as owning gender equality, and Islam is portrayed as being essentially patriarchal and opposed to gender equality. This view assumes that gender equality is a Western idea, as if countries that are described as Western are somehow free of patriarchy. This reductive characterization of both the West and Islam also fails to recognize the diversity and complexity of a globalized world, in which people embody multiple identities. In doing so, this perspective privileges patriarchal Islam as normative and "true" while rejecting as inauthentic the beliefs and practices of hundreds of millions of Muslims who believe that Islam is inherently gender-egalitarian.

Apart from delegitimizing Muslim feminists as inauthentic, cultural relativist liberals accuse Muslim feminists of "self-hate" and "anti-communitarianism." They see Muslim feminists as "insider informants" who have internalized a Western hegemonic ideology and who are imposing Western standards and values on others without respecting the distinct values of various cultures. Muslim feminists are accused of advancing a "culturalist" critique, such that by interrogating internal debates, Muslim feminists are seen as damaging the religion of Islam itself and thus as falling into the clutches of anti-Islamic, colonialist, and imperialist forces. This critique is paradoxical because in critiquing Muslim feminists, cultural relativist liberals must make a truth claim about the essence of Islam, and that truth claim is that Islam is essentially patriarchal and that any expression of a gender-equal Islam is an imposition of Western values on Islam. These liberals see themselves as open-minded enough not only to tolerate but also to respect patriarchal expressions of Islam. Though such liberals would themselves never want to live under such an expression of Islam, they can suspend their moral judgment enough to see that other women might yearn to live under gender-discriminatory laws.

Colonialism and imperialism continue to be important aspects of the cultural relativist critique of Muslim feminists. It is important to be sensitive to and cognizant of the ways that various forms of colonialism and imperialism have harmed Muslim societies by introducing global structures of inequality that continue to oppress the Global South through pernicious military, economic, political, and cultural means. Nevertheless, colonialism and imperialism can and often are summoned to justify and excuse patriarchal interpretations of Islamic laws in Muslim-majority nation-states. Rather than holding contemporary Muslims responsible and accountable for gender-discriminatory interpretations of Islamic law, cultural relativists excuse oppressive practices because Muslims suffered from colonialism and now are suffering from imperialism. We ought to cut them some slack, the argument goes, and marginalized Muslim communities in the West are demonized enough as it is, so we should avoid highlighting the problems of patriarchal expressions of Islam because it confirms existing stereotypes that lead to their further disenfranchisement.

In this critique, colonialism and imperialism are used to sidestep the issue of gender equality. The absolute privileging of a discourse about larger structures of inequality—which certainly deserves our attention—can amount to excusing patriarchal religious abuses of power and to suppressing critiques of such abuse. So, instead of speaking about Muslim religious discourse on domestic violence—which has resulted in many Muslim-majority countries refusing to criminalize domestic violence—cultural relativist liberals prefer we think about domestic violence as a universal problem, emphasizing that it is not restricted to Islam and Muslims. While it is true that gender inequality, domestic violence, and violence against women are universal problems that merit our attention, it is also true that religious reasoning is used to deny Muslim women equal rights, to justify domestic violence, and to encourage "honor" killings in specific Muslim-majority and -minority contexts. Many Muslim-majority nation-states enshrine patriarchal interpretations of Islam in their legislature, protecting the right of husbands to physically discipline their wives in their penal and personal status codes. The fact that the majority of the countries at the bottom of the UN index of gender equality are Muslim-majority countries suggests that Muslim women disproportionately suffer the consequences of patriarchal interpretations of Islam, and when they challenge such interpretations by championing a gender-equal Islam, they are accused of imposing Western values on Islam. In the end, such critiques erase the multiplicity of Muslim experiences and deny the authenticity of Muslim feminists; such a critique cannot grasp the idea that a Muslim woman's demand for equal rights might emerge from a non-Western source and/or that it might be an "authentically Muslim" claim.

Demanding that we focus on the universal problem of gender inequality and violence against women when religious feminists speak about religiously based arguments that support gender inequality and violence against women is, in the end, just as imperialistic, superior, and privileged a move as insisting that gender inequality and violence against women are a uniquely Muslim problem. Both claims are made from the luxurious distance of theoretical rhetoric and ignore the voices of Muslim women speaking up for their own rights. These are the women who stand to lose the most in this debate, and they are the potential and real victims of religiously sanctioned violence. To consider this problem more practically, let us take the examples of Malala Yousafzai and Nabila Rehman. As most people know, the fifteen-year-old Malala Yousafzai was shot in the face by a Taliban gunman because she advocated for girls' and children's education in Pakistan.[18] The lesser-known eight-year-old Nabila Rehman saw her grandmother killed and her siblings injured when a US drone bombed them while they were picking okra.[19] Whereas

---
[18] Ayesha S. Chaudhry, "Malala Yousufzai," in *Encyclopedia of Islam and the Muslim World*, 2nd ed., ed. Richard C. Martin (New York: Macmillan Reference, 2016).
[19] Murtaza Hussain, "Malala and Nabila: Worlds Apart," *Al-Jazeera*, November 1, 2013, http://m.aljazeera.com/story/201311193857549913.

Malala has since received a great deal of attention in Western countries, most recently winning the Nobel Peace Prize, Nabila and her parents were largely ignored when they arrived in Washington, DC, in 2013 to testify at a congressional hearing. Only 5 of the 435 congressional representatives showed up to hear her testimony.

Liberals correctly point out that it is easier for Americans to support Malala because she was attacked by a US enemy, whereas support for Nabila is less forthcoming because it means taking responsibility and being self-critical; it is far easier to criticize a barbaric other than to hold ourselves accountable for the devastating consequences of US foreign policy. However, some liberals have gone further to denigrate anyone who advocates for Malala and to critique Malala herself for focusing simplistically on girls' education in Pakistan while overlooking global structures of inequality. But does this mean that because Malala's cause is more palatable and in line with Western political interests, she ought not receive our support and advocacy? Can we assume that US drones in Pakistan are worth greater resistance and rebuke than governments that deny girls education? Should we privilege the story of Malala over the story of Nabila, or vice versa? The human faces of Malala and Nabila help us see that each oppressive act—whether the result of US foreign policy that kills innocent civilians with drones, or patriarchal interpretations of Islam that drive the Taliban to ban girls from school—deserves our moral outrage, academic attention, and political activism. Neither plight can be denigrated; we cannot explain away one problem as the product of colonialism while privileging the other as the real problem at hand. We cannot say that because Malala's voice is more palatable to a Western audience and can be used to play into Islamophobia, it ought to be suppressed or ignored. We should not say that Nabila's story is morally superior only because it avoids tropes. Making any of these claims is precisely orientalist and dehumanizing of the experience of Pakistanis on the ground.

The debates around Muslim feminisms are not unique. Sociologists use the terms *culturalist* and *structuralist* to describe the opposing positions in this debate.[20] When looking at the problem of pervasive patriarchy in Muslim societies, culturalists will "emphasize the self-perpetuating norms and behaviors" that make patriarchy so pervasive in Muslim communities. They take Muslim agency seriously when considering why Muslims legislate gender-discriminatory laws in Muslim-majority countries and why women are segregated and discriminated against in the majority of mosques in Muslim-minority settings. Structuralists, in contrast, "emphasize the role of institutional racism and economic circumstances."[21] According to structuralists, focusing on Muslim agency when thinking about the pervasive nature of patriarchy in Muslim religious and social structures is tantamount to missing the forest for the trees, since patriarchy is a human problem that manifests itself in every human society in various ways. Furthermore, structuralists argue that we cannot critique the laws of a particular nation-state without taking into account that nation-state's position in the web of global power structures. In the debate about religious feminisms, each approach—both culturalist and structuralist—critiques the other; culturalists believe that structuralists ignore the plight of actual living women advocating for their rights from within a specific religious and political framework, while structuralists critique culturalists for "victim blaming," arguing that Muslim men and women have the right to choose gender discrimination based on alternative values. They think of "Muslims" rather than only "Muslim women" as the "real" victims in this exchange of power.[22]

---

[20] For representatives of the culturalist approach, see Daniel P. Moynihan, *The Negro Family: The Case for National Action* (Washington, DC: Office of Policy Planning and Research, US Department of Labor, 1965); and Orlando Patterson and Ethan Foss, eds., *The Cultural Matrix: Understanding Black Youth* (Cambridge, MA: Harvard University Press, 2015); For representatives of the structuralist approach, see Andrew Billingsley, *Black Families and the Struggle for Survival* (New York: Friendship, 1974); and William Ryan, *Blaming the Victim* (New York: Vintage, 1972).

[21] Kelefa Sanneh, "Don't Be Like That: Does Black Culture Need to Be Reformed?" *New Yorker*, February 9, 2015, 62–68. He brought up these approaches in relation to the debate about African Americans.

[22] Tommie Shelby, "Liberalism, Self-Respect, and Troubling Cultural Patterns in Ghettos," in Patterson and Foss, *Cultural Matrix*.

The fact of the matter is that both the structuralist and culturalist approaches add valuable perspectives to any debate; they are not mutually exclusive and ought to be considered together. We know that in the debate about Muslim feminisms, Muslims must be held accountable for legislating gender-discriminatory laws and for creating mosque spaces that disempower or sideline women. At the same time, these discussions happen in political contexts, in which feminism is highly politicized. Each of these approaches in isolation can devolve into racist and dehumanizing tropes. If we see patriarchy as exclusively Muslim, then we essentialize Islam and Muslims as a dehumanized other; this line of thinking is Islamophobic. At the same time, focusing solely on the universal nature of patriarchy or on the disempowered position of Muslims globally ignores Muslim agency as well as the voices of Muslim feminists calling for gender reform in Muslim communities. This line of thinking also dehumanizes Muslims as the other. Each approach, in isolation, sets up a good Muslim-bad Muslim binary that makes a claim about who are the "good" and "bad" Muslims. According to culturalists, the good Muslim is the self-critical Muslim who calls out "Islamic patriarchy" and stands up to "bad" Muslims, and bad Muslims are conservative Muslims who do not follow a particular narrow definition of "liberal." For structuralists, the good Muslim is the one who maintains precolonial Muslim ideals of patriarchy against the hegemony of Western values defined broadly, while the bad Muslim is the one who tries to reform Muslim communities through self-critical intra-Muslim engagement.

In contrast, what makes the Muslim feminist critique especially valuable is that it is culturalist and structuralist at once; it recognizes Muslim agency and holds Muslims accountable for the patriarchal expressions of this agency in both majority and minority contexts. Using the theoretical framework of intersectionality, Muslim feminists refuse to see Muslims as pure victims; rather, they see Muslims as always standing at an intersection of various influences, enacting their own power and being acted upon by the power of others. When the Muslim feminist critique occurs in a Muslim-majority context in which religious reasoning is used to justify gender-discriminatory laws, the critique is simultaneously culturalist and structuralist. Muslim feminists denounce the state's use of religious reasoning to justify gender discrimination, as well as religious reasoning that upholds such discrimination; in this case, they call for a reform of both religious reasoning and state law. In contexts where Muslims are a minority, Muslim feminists also make a culturalist and structuralist critique; their culturalist critique is that Muslims ought not to set up religious structures that discriminate against women and, further, that these expressions of Islam are inauthentic. In this context also, religious thinking and the way it is captured in organized religious structures must be reformed to be gender-equal.

In the end, the problem with cultural relativist liberalism and patriarchal interpretations of Islam is that both posit a binary between Islam and the West that is essentialist and reductive. Both lines of reasoning reject the beliefs of hundreds of millions of Muslims who believe that Islam and gender equality are fully compatible. At the same time, both privilege patriarchal interpretations of Islam as authentically Islamic, or representing "true" Islam. Upholding this essentialist binary can only be done at the expense of dehumanizing Muslims, especially Muslim women, who are seen as not desiring basic human rights and gender equality, despite repeated and consistent demands by Muslim women for equal rights. Muslim women are somehow seen to not desire the very same rights that "Western" women demand in liberal democracies; when they do so, their voices are dismissed as representations of "false consciousness," that is, believing that they desire something when in fact that desire is manufactured through an internalization of colonialist discourse.

If we replace gender with race in this conversation, the patronizing, dehumanizing, and orientalist nature of these positions quickly becomes clear.²³ Imagine the dehumanization that would be necessary to make the argument that some races prefer slavery or are not obsessed with equality as found in Western human rights discourses. Suppose those advocating for the abolishment of slavery in Mauritania were charged with importing Western values onto a Muslim population and that shedding light on the extent and character of slavery in Mauritania was a problem because it confirmed Islamophobic stereotypes about Muslims. More provocatively, think about how this conversation maps onto the sort of "Islamic law" that Da'esh claims to be instituting in its strongholds. Is criticism of their interpretation of Islamic law a Western intervention? Is it only a Western intervention when we critique their treatment of women and not when we critique their attempts to bring slavery back, or their treatment of hostages? Muslim feminists occupy the space in between this false binary of Islam and West, and in doing so, their very existence demonstrates the falseness of that binary, evoking the wrath of Muslims who champion a patriarchal Islam, as well as cultural relativist liberals.

What's in a Name?

Let us now return to the first critique that I encounter from my interlocutors, the critique about nomenclature. One of the most powerful tools available to Muslim feminists when formulating their arguments is language; Muslim feminists challenge patriarchal interpretations of Islam and posit new interpretations through writing and speaking. In particular, they explicitly identify particular lines of

---

²³ Consider Shelly Matthews's paper in this volume, in which she draws our attention to kyriarchy, which emphasizes the connection between various oppressions, such as gender and race ("To Be One and the Same with the Woman Whose Head Is Shaven: Resisting the Violence of 1 Corinthians 11:2–16 from the Bottom of the Kyriarchal Pyramid," chapter 2).

reasoning as patriarchal or abusive. Naming violence is an essential part of the fight to combat violence; one cannot combat violence until it has been named. Humans have recognized and wrestled with the power in the act of naming for eternity. A quick comparison of the terms *freedom fighters* to *terrorists*, of *collateral damage* to *innocent victims,*" and of *wife beating* to *physical discipline* illustrates the political nature of naming. Here, I would like to use the Qur'anic story of the creation of Adam (2:30–34) to explore the power wielded by the agent who is vested with the capacity to name. I will paraphrase the story here from a feminist perspective, paying close attention to how power is structured in the story by relying on what Elisabeth Schüssler Fiorenza calls the "hermeneutics of suspicion."[24]

The scene is set in a conversation between God and the angels, in which God makes a dramatic announcement. She has decided to create a vicegerent for herself on Earth. The angels are dismayed by this news. Instead of praising God, they doubt her decision, asking, "Will You place upon [Earth] one who causes corruption therein and sheds blood, while we declare Your praise and sanctify You?" Although the angels claim that they only praise and sanctify God, this is not how they respond to God's announcement to create Adam. Rather, they are extremely critical and question God's decision. God does not engage their criticism, neither the assumed corruption of the as-yet uncreated vicegerent nor the representation of the angels as creatures devoted to praising and sanctifying God. She answers simply, "Indeed, I know that which you do not know."

God goes ahead and creates the vicegerent, names him Adam, and then teaches him "the names of all things." With this knowledge, Adam is increased in stature and becomes superior to the angels. To demonstrate Adam's superiority, God stages an encounter between the angels and Adam. She presents the "named things" to the angels

---

[24] Elisabeth Shüssler Fiorenza, *Sharing Her Word: Feminist Biblical Interpretation in Context* (Edinburgh: Beacon, 1998), 88–90.

and commands, "Inform Me of the names of these, if you are truthful." The angels respond, "We have no knowledge except what You have taught us." God then turns to Adam and instructs him to "inform them of their names." He does this—which does not seem too difficult, since he was taught the names—and God says, "Did I not tell you that I know the unseen of the heavens and the earth?" This is an odd test: God has stacked the cards against the angels by teaching Adam the "names of all things" while withholding information from the angels that they need to pass the test.

Still, the test seems to demonstrate Adam's superiority to the angels, a point that is driven home by God's command for the angels to prostrate to Adam. All the angels obey God and prostrate to Adam, except for one character, named Iblīs. Why does Iblīs refuse to prostrate? Does he object to Adam's authority? Does he disagree with the names? Does he believe the test was not fair to begin with? Does he contest Adam's authority despite his ability to name "all things"? Iblīs's reason is not mentioned, but whatever the reason, Iblīs's refusal incurs God's wrath, and Iblīs is banished from paradise and demonized, renamed Satan. He is thereafter described as an "arrogant disbeliever." For a time, Adam and his wife dwell in paradise, but eventually, they too are expelled to Earth and enter an epic and eternal battle with Satan.

In this story, the act of naming vindicates God's decision to create a vicegerent. In fact, it is in the act of naming, as God has taught him, that Adam becomes God's vicegerent. In acquiring the power of naming, Adam becomes more Godlike and less angel-like, he is imbued with God's authority. The strangeness of God's test draws our attention to the power of the angels in this story. Though at first glance it may seem that they have no power and that God does as she pleases, a closer look reveals that God appears to need the approval of the angels, for whatever reason. The power of the angels is first expressed in their critique of God's decision to create Adam. Rather than praising God's decision as brilliant, they are highly critical, advising God to abandon her plans. Their power is also expressed in God's need for the angels to accept Adam's superiority over them, by having them prostrate to Adam. Finally, the power of the angels is demonstrated by God's demonization of Iblīs. Rather than ignore his refusal, God makes an example out of him.

Iblīs's refusal to prostrate to Adam does Adam real harm by catapulting them both into an eternal battle. What harm would have come to Adam had all the angels refused to prostrate to him? And would the angels have prostrated to Adam had he not known the names of all things, if Adam had not dominated them by his power of naming, even if this domination came to be by means of a rigged test in which Adam had an obvious advantage? The angels seem to know that the test was rigged (they say, "We have no knowledge except what You have taught us"), but they still bow down to Adam. In this light, their acquiescence to Adam's superiority becomes a pragmatic choice. Perhaps they realize that God has thrown her weight behind Adam, so refusing to prostrate to him would have terrible consequences for them, and Iblīs's demonization and banishment at the hands of God for refusing to bow down to Adam proves that the angels made the correct pragmatic choice in terms of self-preservation.

Musical Chairs: Adam, Satan, and the Angels

The Islamic creation story is instructive for us as we think about the power and responsibility in naming violence as religious feminists. In constructing gender-egalitarian visions of patriarchal religious traditions, religious feminists must name the inherent violence and oppression of patriarchy. Naming gendered violence is an essential part of the religious feminist project because doing so explains and justifies the project itself. After all, why create a gender-equal vision of a patriarchal religious tradition if that vision does no harm?

A question that all religious feminists must confront is, how do we name violence without God's voice directly and clearly teaching us the names of violent and oppressive acts? And how do we name violence without God setting up a stage for us to demonstrate our knowledge of these names?

Of the three characters in the story—Adam, the angels, and Iblīs—who are we most like? Are we Adam-like, possessing the knowledge and resulting authority of knowing and speaking the correct names? If so, how can we do this without Adam's certainty in learning the names from God Herself? Or ought we be like the angels, who do not name anything themselves but lend their power to Adam, whose superiority they accept? In bowing to Adam, the angels avoid the trouble and drama that Adam and Iblīs eventually find themselves in, both expelled to Earth, but they also make themselves irrelevant to the unfolding drama. And what of Iblīs-turned-Satan? Iblīs asserts his power in rejecting the significance of naming, using his power to challenge the names and the resulting authority. He accepts the consequence—expulsion and demonization by God Herself—that results from his refusal to prostrate to God's new creation. Iblīs's role in the story is essential; it calls our attention to the fact that names are not fixed, are inherently changeable, and often change depending on one's relationship with power. In the end, both Adam and Iblīs are expelled to Earth; Adam's knowledge of the names does not save him from expulsion.

Let us return to the critiques I encounter as a Muslim feminist: the critique of misnaming and of Western hegemonic imperialism. If we use the story of Adam as a metaphor for my relationship with my interlocutors, who am I and who are my critics? I would like to believe that I am Adam, naming domestic violence as a first step to contesting religious rhetoric that justifies such violence. I would like to use the power of naming to protect Muslim women from religiously sanctioned domestic violence. If I am Adam, then my patriarchal coreligionists are Iblīs. They uphold a violent interpretation of

Qur'an 4:34 and protect their religious tradition over and against living women who suffer the consequences of religiously sanctioned violence. They believe Islam and the West to be discrete and mutually exclusive entities, in which gender equality is Western and therefore incompatible with Islam. But I am acutely aware that my coreligionists who promote patriarchal interpretations of Islam think of themselves as Adam and me as Iblīs.

In the creation story, Iblīs's key characteristic is that he refuses to bow down to the Adam who can name all things. In my view, my patriarchal coreligionists are refusing to prostrate and submit to a just, gender-egalitarian interpretation of Islam. Instead, they are displaying arrogance by maintaining the patriarchal status quo despite my naming the violence that comes with patriarchy. In their view, however, it is I refusing to prostrate and submit to the Islamic tradition and displaying arrogance by not giving up my quest for a gender-egalitarian Islam and accepting an Islam that treats men and women as inherently different creations of God. Adam and Iblīs fundamentally disagree about the names of things and will always be opposed to one another. Each thinks himself to be correct; most importantly, each believes himself to be Adam and the other to be Iblīs, sometimes demonizing the other as Satan. Indeed, a co-panelist at an academic conference held at an elite university unironically described my scholarship as a representation of the "hermeneutics of Satan."

The angels, in the scenario wherein I am Iblīs and my patriarchal coreligionists are Adam, are cultural relativist liberals and supercessionist feminists who believe that there is a dichotomy between Islam and gender egalitarianism, that gender egalitarianism is Western while Islam is inherently patriarchal, but not because of their commitment to a patriarchal Islam. They see Muslim feminists as imposing—justifiably or not—a hegemonic Western discourse on a patriarchal religious tradition. In seeing Muslim feminists as relying on Western values to create a gender-equal Islam, these liberals affirm the superiority of their Adam (my Iblīs), seeing patriarchal Islam as more authentic. This endorsement has political consequences; it makes claims about the "true" nature of Islam; it privileges the most patriarchal expressions of Islam as the "real" Islam and casts Muslim feminists as Iblīs rather than as Adam.

The contestation about who is playing the role of which character in the creation story results from the absence of a God who can tell us the identity of Adam, Iblīs, and the angels. Nation-states that claim to follow Islamic law or sharia act in place of God; they take on the authority of God and tell us who is Adam and who is Iblīs: Religious scholars who endorse the state's interpretation of Islam are Adam, and those who critique the state's representation of God's law are Iblīs. Because the state acts as a stand-in for God, the state demonizes Iblīs as Satan. This means that Muslim feminists, who offer culturalist and structuralist critiques of the state by accusing the state of misrepresenting and misapplying God's law on its citizens, often find themselves demonized by both the state and patriarchal Muslims.

Who Dares Name Satan?

If we dig deeper into the Qur'anic story of Adam, we see that this is not so much the story of the creation of humans but of the creation of an eternal relational struggle between three character types: Adam, the angels, and Iblīs. Though the story externalizes each character as a discrete entity, it is more likely that each of us embodies all three character types simultaneously. We have it within our power to embody aspects of each character, and we have the power to identify others as Adam, Iblīs, and the angels, but one thing we know for certain is that none of us—neither patriarchal Muslims, nor Muslim feminists, nor cultural relativist liberals—is God.

This means that none of us has absolute knowledge about the identity of ourselves or others. Hence, none of us ought to demonize the other. Only God can demonize Iblīs by naming him Satan, and in the Qur'anic creation story, even this demonization can be read as morally problematic. This is all the more reason for the rest of us not to demonize each other. We all play the role of Adam, the angels, and Iblīs in various contexts, depending on our relationships with power. In the political and religious discourse of Islamic feminism, it is important for each of us to be more self-reflective of our positionalities. Each of us makes our claims about Islam from a particular position of power; there is no neutral, disinterested position in this debate. At this historical moment, the "true" nature of Islam, whether patriarchal or gender-egalitarian, is deeply contested. Given this, the positions we take and the arguments we deem (il)legitimate are necessarily political.

As a Muslim feminist, I am troubled by the critique of my positionality by both patriarchal Muslims and cultural relativist liberals. Because gender is the most contested aspect of Islam at the moment, it makes perfect sense that Muslims disagree with each other about the "true" nature of Islam. It is not the disagreement that is problematic, however; what is troublesome is the way this disagreement is expressed. The fact that patriarchal Muslims see Muslim feminists as Iblīs is understandable. What is unacceptable is the tendency for patriarchal Muslims to conflate Iblīs with Satan and, instead of engaging the ideas of Muslim feminists and explaining why they disagree with them, to dismiss Muslim feminists and their ideas through demonization. The common questions about the sincerity of Muslim feminists, the fear of the Trojan horse, the accusation of Muslim feminists colluding with imperialist powers, all sidestep substantive issues raised by Muslim feminists. Ultimately, Muslim feminists are asking for something very basic; we are demanding that patriarchal Muslims such as Qadhi extend us the same courtesy they would to other Muslims with whom they disagree. This is a courtesy that patriarchal Muslims are willing to extend even to Muslims groups such as ISIS. Because patriarchal Muslims are willing to engage the religious arguments of ISIS and express their disagreement in religious language, why not do the same with Muslim feminists?[25]

The angels (cultural relativist liberals) must accept the agency and the power that they have in this drama, and see that Muslims are deeply divided on the issue of gender equality in Islam. One position is not more or less authentic, more Muslim or Western than the other. The angels in this scenario often conflate those Muslims who champion theocratic and authoritarian expressions of Islamic law with authentic, "true" Islam. Muslim feminists challenge this conflation and the resulting truth claim that the most patriarchal expressions of Islam are truly Islamic. They would prefer that cultural-relativist liberals make a more considered choice about whom they will name Adam and Iblīs. The position that cultural relativist liberals take can do Muslim feminists real harm; it can further compromise Muslim feminists' position when they are already in danger of being expelled from their communities and nation-states. In this compromised position, Muslim feminists must defend their Islamic sincerity to those who accuse them of heresy, and they must also defend their position against cultural relativist liberals who question the authenticity of their critique. This is a frustrating and, frankly, annoying position to find oneself in and demonstrates the hubris that often accompanies cultural relativism. The angels can also do Muslim feminists real good, however; they can help change the discourse by turning a critical gaze on patriarchal interpretations of Islam to expose the political and opportunistic role of such interpretations in Muslim communities, and see this patriarchal impulse as part of the broader problem of patriarchy

---

[25] At time of the writing of this article, patriarchal Muslim scholars met in Dubai to discuss extremism, and Grand Sheikh Ahmed Al Tayyeb, of Al Azhar University "called the forum to collect literature and media publications issued by terrorist groups to counter their arguments" (accessed September 21, 2015, http://www.thenational.ae/uae/outdated-religious-laws-must-be-changed-uae-forum-hears). There has yet to be a forum in which scholars convene to seriously address the concerns of Muslim feminists.

with which feminists of all stripes must contend in their quest for equality.

Ultimately, Muslims disagree about the nature of Islam and its views on gender equality and patriarchy. Some Muslims argue that Islam is fundamentally patriarchal, while others assert that it is essentially gender-egalitarian. In claiming that Islam is gender-egalitarian, Muslim feminists occupy a difficult but ever-growing space, and though they are critiqued from all sides, they have continued to occupy this space for the past few decades and their ranks have increased rather than diminished. As we begin to get a bit more comfortable in this difficult space, we can take a moment to breathe and think through some of the critiques we encounter, and can use religious resources to articulate a theological position that engages with the ideas of our interlocutors. Though this intellectual engagement will not erase our differences, it does allow us to define the contours of the difficult space in which we live and to articulate, in religious terms, why this space is one of dignity, sincerity, and moral probity.

CHAPTER 6

Gang-Raped and Dis-Membered: Contextual Biblical Study of Judges 19:1–30 to Re-Member the Rwandan Genocide

Fulata Lusungu Moyo

I saw her body distinct from the other bodies sharing the display table with her. Though desiccated, the corpse still reflected the painful death she must have experienced, her thighs wide apart, arms akimbo, and face still expressive of the painful scream that must have inevitably escaped her as she endured such horror at the hands of her rapists and killers. She spoke to me, naming her painful death, breaking the silence around both her sexual violation and her equally traumatic death. I stood in front of her in a sacred space at a sacred moment. "How did she die?" I asked our guide, pointing in awed reverence at her remains. As the guide related her story, the horror and fear that the remains of her facial expression conveyed triggered a fast pumping of blood into my heart, bringing my own past sizzling pain alive.[1]

---

[1] This was at Murambi genocide museum near Gikongoro, Rwanda, Africa, where at least eight hundred corpses have been preserved and left untouched just as they died. These bodies are displayed in burial rooms, and some bodies have been buried outside these burial rooms. I was part of a team of Christians, theologians, a documentary producer, a publisher, and a lawyer accompanying a Rwandan couple who had survived the genocide and witnessed most of their family cruelly massacred by people they had grown up with. This couple had invited us to a pilgrimage of reflection and prayer, searching the meaning of where God was when all these atrocities were happening. Was God there amid hatred and violence? Where was God when twenty or so militia men raped each woman, occasionally dismembered one, and even infected them with HIV? Judges 19 became the core of my reflections. A short documentary was produced: *Return to Rwanda: A Journey of Hope* (https://vimeo.com/90597947).

As often happens when my own sexual abuse is remembered in another's experience, emotions flooded me and resulted in a sudden stream of tears. While I was witnessing this woman's pain and remembering my own, the similar story of a woman gang-raped and dismembered that the Hebrew Bible recounts in Judges 19:1–30 spontaneously came alive. Looking at this violated woman, I had an epiphany of real embodiment. Three women from different contexts, two from the same generation, had an encounter of solidarity. The nameless woman only colloquially known as the Levite's concubine, the raped Rwandan woman whose name and life story dried up with the remains of her body, and myself, who had been violated at age nine by a male cousin nine years older, had a cross-generational spiritual connection of contempt.

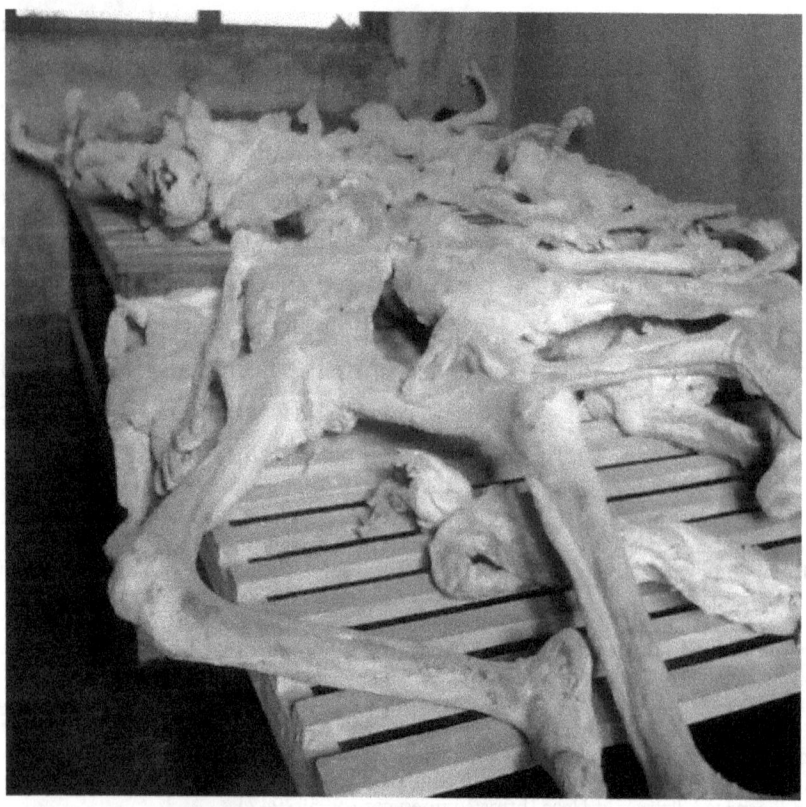

Corpse in Burial Room, Murambi Genocide Memorial Center

The memory and image of the first two women urged me to name them and to advocate for the end of sexual violence. So many questions arose within me: What really is it about being a woman that makes us easy targets of such dehumanization even within most sacred contexts? What has changed between the concubine's dehumanization and the rape and murder of our Rwandan sisters more than two thousand years later? How can this nameless sister—the Levite's concubine—help us bring awareness and advocate for a world without sexual and gender-based violence when religion and its sacred texts are still manipulated to justify the dehumanization of women?

In this essay, I use Judges 19 as "sacred witness" (in the words of Old Testament scholar Susanne Scholz[2]) to the dehumanizing reality of sexual violence rooted and sustained by certain ethical practices such as hospitality. Reading Judges 19 using contextual Bible study (CBS) methodology turns this story into "a pedagogical tool that strengthens our ability to confront sexual violence."[3] By reading the story of the Levite's concubine through the lens of CBS, we can name sexual violence as a crime that no human community should ever accept, and thereby set in motion a process of breaking the silence that often surrounds such violations and of working out possible actions to end sexual and gender-based violence.

The CBS interaction in this case is between Judges 19:1–30 and the context of sexually violated Rwandan women and girls. The Levite's concubine is embodied in the unknown raped Rwandan woman and through my own experience as a survivor of sexual violence. How does the Levite's concubine speak to both of us? What are

---

[2] Susanne Scholz, *Sacred Witness: Rape in the Hebrew Bible* (Minneapolis, MN: Fortress, 2010), 209.
[3] Angelina Duell, "Judges 19: The Levite's Concubine—Constructing a Hermeneutics of Meaning for Victims/Survivors of Sexual Violence," April 20, 2014, https://www.academia.edu/633135/Judges_19_The_Levites_Concubine_-_Constructing_a_Hermeneutics_of_Meaning_for_Victim_Survivors_of_Sexual_Violence.

the similarities and differences of our experiences as well as the ethical practices surrounding them? How can this embodiment help break the silence around and name sexual violence as blasphemy against the God who created women and men?

The reading of Judges 19 as a gruesome text that spells out sexual and gender-based violence is part of our call to read all sacred texts through the lens of our academic and religious orientations as a means by which to combat violence against women. As biblical scholar and peace activist Sarra Lev explains, Judges 19 summons us to seek out its holiness.[4]

Breaking the Silence through Contextual Bible Study

CBS emphasizes reading biblical texts within a community that searches for solutions to painful realities afflicting its members. CBS creates a space and an atmosphere in which the context of the community can dialogue with the context of the biblical narrative to raise awareness and to act for transformation and liberation.

The facilitator of the Bible study chooses the biblical text according to the community's needs and formulates questions using exegesis and interpretation as critical tools that help unveil meaning. CBS practitioners formulate questions that adhere to the liberational pedagogical process of see, judge, and act. Practitioners formulate questions that adopt the writer's perspective, raise community consciousness, challenge the community to work toward addressing their needs, and serve as a call for advocacy.

CBS is rooted in liberation theologies, including feminist liberation theology. It is formulated from the hermeneutics of suspicion with the acknowledgment that sacred texts are often written from the

---

[4] Sarra Lev, "'Dipping a Finger in Honey': Sensemaking in the Face of Violent Texts," (chapter 3).

context of male privilege. Such a patriarchal—or, more appropriately, kyriarchal[5]—mindset presents sacred texts from the point of view of those who benefit from such a system and advocates for stereotypical gender roles. Like feminist liberation theologians, CBS practitioners raise "So what?" questions that spur the community to take action about the situation they face and for which the Bible study was developed and facilitated. Take, for example, the text of Judges 19:1–2, 25–30, which reads:

> In those days, when there was no king in Israel, a certain Levite, residing in the remote parts of the hill country of Ephraim, took to himself a concubine from Bethlehem in Judah. But his concubine became angry with him, and she went away from him to her father's house at Bethlehem in Judah, and was there some four months.

The Levite who brought with him servants and horses is said to have stayed for several days before he could return, for every time he wanted to set off, the father of the nameless woman I will contextually call Suzgika ("the troubled one" in Malawian Tumbuka language) convinced him to spend one more day, until the fifth day. The Levite left when the day was almost spent. He refused to spend a night in Jebus because it was a city of foreigners, but decided to spend a night near Gibeah, which belonged to Benjamin. There, an old Benjamite man offered the Levite and his concubine hospitality in his home. That night, the men of the town surrounded the house, and demanded that the old man give them the Levite so they could gang-rape him. The host protected the man but offered his own virgin daughter and the Levite's concubine, Suzgika, instead:

---

[5] For a definition of *kyriarchy*, as to rule and dominate, see Elisabeth Schüssler Fiorenza, *Changing Horizons: Explorations in Feminist Interpretation* (Minneapolis, MN: Fortress, 2013), 7.

> So the man seized his concubine, and put her out to them. They wantonly raped her, and abused her all through the night until the morning. And as the dawn began to break, they let her go. As morning appeared, the woman came and fell down at the door of the man's house where her master was, until it was light. . . . . When he had entered his house, he took a knife, and grasping his concubine he cut her into twelve pieces, limb by limb, and sent her throughout all the territory of Israel. Then he commanded the men whom he sent, saying, "Thus shall you say to all the Israelites, 'Has such a thing ever happened since the day that the Israelites came up from the land of Egypt until this day?' Consider it, take counsel, and speak out."[6]

Reading Judges 19 through CBS helps create a space where this horrific story can be used to speak to similar realities within its reading community. CBS enables and encourages readers to engage directly with disturbing texts and does not perpetuate the conspiracy of silence that often surrounds these texts and the issues they raise.

Similar to Islam and gender scholar Ayesha Chaudhry's call to postcolonial nonviolent reading of sacred texts for gender justice,[7] our CBS reading of Judges 19 embraces a non-imperial lens so even violent texts like this one can be "transformed" into witnesses for the quest for gender justice and peace. Unlike Qur'an 4:34, which has often been read to justify a husband's beating of his wife as discipline, it would take more than colonial patriarchal reading of Judges 19 to

---

[6] "Judges 19:1–30," *The New Oxford Annotated Bible. An Ecumenical Study Bible*, New Revised Standard Version (New York: Oxford University Press, 2001), 384–86.

[7] Ayesha S. Chaudhry, "Naming Violence: Quran Interpretation between Social Justice and Cultural Relativism," (paper presented the Annual Meeting of the Society for Biblical Literature, San Diego, California, November 22, 2014), and Ayesha S. Chaudhry, *Domestic Violence and the Islamic Tradition: Ethics, Law, and the Muslim Discourse on Gender* (New York: Oxford University Press, 2013).

justify what the host or the guest (Levite) did in sacrificing the "concubine" to be gang-raped and then cut up into twelve pieces.

CBS helps unlock horrific doors by allowing this story, as one of feminist biblical scholar Phyllis Trible's "texts of terror," to bring to life current realities and to name sexual violence as an injustice and evil done to this woman.[8] CBS articulates the silence around such an oppression and spurs the community to work out praxis for justice and peace. Using CBS also helps illuminate current living stories that are often suppressed in the conspiracy of silent shame. In the case of the Rwandan twentieth-anniversary remembrance (1994–2014), this kind of reading then helps reveal the experience of gang rape that was part of the Rwandan genocide—the biblical nameless woman in Judges 19:1–30 becomes embodied in the current stories of victims of sexual violence and murder through raped and killed Rwandan women.

Gang-Raped and Dis-Membered: Re-Membering Raped Rwandan Women

During the Rwandan genocide (approximately April 6–July 16, 1994), at least one million Tutsis and moderate Hutus were murdered; a significant number of these casualties were women who were raped before they were murdered.[9] The opening image of this article is an example of the many women and girls who suffered such double and terminal dehumanization. Another estimated 250,000 to 500,000 women were raped but not murdered. In a

---

[8] Phyllis Trible, *Texts of Terror: Literary-Feminist Readings of Biblical Narratives*, Overtures to Biblical Theology (Minneapolis, MN: Fortress, 1984).
[9] There is missing data regarding how many women were raped before they were killed. For a detailed discussion on this, see Nancy Sai, "Rwanda," Women under Siege, Women's Media Center, February 8, 2012, http://www.womenundersiegeproject.org/conflicts/profile/rwanda.

planned and systematic genocidal fashion, HIV-positive rapists systematically infected an estimated 67 percent of the raped women with HIV.[10]

These mass rapes are alleged to have been carried out by the Interahamwe militia, Rwandan military, Rwandan Presidential Guards, and members of the civilian population. As is the case in many conflict situations, rape was used as a weapon of genocide—women's bodies became part of the battlefield. The desiccated corpse pictured above that recalled my own experience of sexual violence had been just one of the many Rwandan women who suffered such dehumanization. Jean Bosco Rutagengwa—husband to Christine, and one half of the couple that seven colleagues and friends and I had the honor of accompanying in Rwanda in December 2013 on what they and we considered to be a pilgrimage of resurrection—shared one of the many horror stories of rape victims. When he had been exchanged and arrived on the "safe" side of the Rwandan Resistance Army, he saw one woman's body leaning on a bench among the many massacred and still unburied bodies.[11] Her clothes were torn and her feet and arms were spread—evidence of her having been raped before being killed by a machete. Even as he recounted the story twenty years later, the wrinkles on Rutagengwa's face and the tears in his eyes expressed pain he could not hide.

These atrocities happened among Hutus and Tutsis, whose cultures, prior to the conflict, valued hospitality, lived with each other as

---

[10] Binaifer Nowrojee, *Shattered Lives: Sexual Violence during the Rwandan Genocide and Its Aftermath.* (Human Rights Watch, 1996); and Binaifer Nowrojee, "A Lost Opportunity for Justice: Why Did the ICTR Not Prosecute Gender Propaganda?" in *The Media and the Rwandan Genocide,* ed. Allan Thompson (London: Pluto, 2007), 362–74.

[11] When the Rwandan Patriotic Front (RPF) under Paul Kagame invaded the Rwandan capital, Kigali, one of the agreements was to exchange "genocide prisoners." Jean Bosco and Christine were some of the prisoners successfully exchanged from Kigali to the side that the RPF fully controlled. RPF defeated the Rwandan government forces in Kigali on July 4, 1994. For details, see Romeo Dallaire, *Shake Hands with the Devil: The Failure of Humanity in Rwanda* (New York: Random House, 2003). See also various articles on Rwanda at Human Rights Watch (https//www.hrw.org).

neighbors, and often were intermarried and belonged to the same churches; yet powerful xenophobic Rwandans treated ethnic differences between the two groups with suspicion, fear, and enmity. According to feminist theologian Letty Russell, "this fear of difference has even been used by those in power as an excuse to oppress those who are different. And churches unfortunately reinforce this fear and rejection by becoming 'safe havens' from difference, welcoming only certain groups."[12]

Like Judges 19, the story of the Rwandan genocide is both an ethnic and a gender power play that articulates how those in power can abuse their standing in society to dictate who is human and who has the right to live. In both the biblical and the Rwandan narratives, women's bodies are expendable weapons in men's power games. While in the Rwandan genocide, women were part of the weapons of ethnic cleansing, in Judges 19, a woman's body is used as a weapon of sexual exploitation in the protection of the Levite, who is a valued guest of the Ephraimite residing in Gibeah. The old man from Ephraim considers the Levite as his real guest deserving protection from the men demanding to have sex with him (the Levite). The old man prefers handing over his virgin daughter to be raped by this gang to having his male guest harmed (Judges 19:23–24). In turn, the Levite's concubine is part of reverse hospitality in that instead of being a guest deserving protection, she is forced to "offer" costly sexual hospitality to a gang of rapists (Judges 19:25–26). She is caught in an interethnic conflict in which sexual and gender-based violence have become intrinsic.

It is impossible to reconcile the Levite's patient negotiation with the father to have his so-called concubine back and his willingness to give her away to the gang of rapists. She was part of the property of men—the father and the Levite lover. As property, she was used to

---

[12] Letty M. Russell, *Just Hospitality: God's Welcome in a World of Difference* (Louisville, KY: Westminster John Knox, 2009), 21.

serve male interests, in this case an appeasement for ethnic conflict in which the early indicators of the reality of rape as a weapon of war were clearly expressed. Her body became the battlefield—gang-raped all night, then cut into twelve pieces by the Levite.

Raped and murdered Rwandan women and girls become an embodiment of the nameless woman in Judges 19, transitioning us into the current realities of sexual and gender-based violence. Such a liberating style of reading helps us raise awareness about such injustices and violation of women's and children's rights so that, together as communities of faith, we can work out actions to end such oppression for a culture of justice and peace with no sexual and gender-based violence.

How should we consider these stories, take counsel, and speak out against the issues they raise? The final chapters of the Judges passage relate the lamentable stories of the battles that ensue between the Benjaminites and the Israelites as the latter sought vengeance for the crime against the concubine woman. Thousands of people are slaughtered, thousands of women are raped, abducted dancers become wives for the Benjaminites, and there is lasting separation between the Benjaminites and the Israelites. It is a story of interethnic chaos, violence, and revenge that sounds all too familiar today as global media outlets drag us through the bloody streets of Ukraine, Syria, Israel and Palestine, Kenya and Somalia, Sudan, Iran, and Iraq, to name only some of the armed conflict areas.

According to John Thompson, apart from a few times when the gang rape was justified as punishment for the woman's sin of prostitution, very little was said about the Levite's concubine until the twentieth century, when scholars began to pay increased attention to the narrative.[13] Today, one might argue that from its start to the time

---

[13] John L. Thompson, *Writing the Wrongs: Women of the Old Testament among Biblical Commentators from Philo through the Reformation* (New York: Oxford University Press, 2001), 201.

when her body is picked up in the morning, the concubine's story can be read as about costly and reversed hospitality (here understood as a form of spirituality in the practice of God's welcome). In its true meaning, hospitality is supposed to reach across differences to allow all humans to participate in God's actions, bringing justice and healing to a world in crisis. Although as a Judeo-Christian imperative, the biblical witness to hospitality is clear (Heb 13:2, Ex 23:9, Matt 25:31–46[14]), it is nevertheless a difficult and challenging call of duty that requires one to be in solidarity with strangers, "others," and those who are "naturally" unlovable. Hospitality involves the care, provision, and protection of the stranger, requiring hosts to ensure that guests are cared for, fed, and housed appropriately.

Hospitality is a complex issue in this story, however, beginning with the Levite traveling to his estranged partner's father's home in Bethlehem. In the biblical context, the concubine is a second wife, not granted the status of a primary wife. Although the Bible does not relate why, the concubine returns to her father's house. Perhaps as a concubine, she was mistreated. After four months apart and hoping to win back the woman's attention, the man travels to Bethlehem, where her father greets him joyfully and wines and dines him for several days.

The father-in-law's urging of the Levite to stay and the Levite's eventual decision to leave late on the fifth day imply a degree of tension. Having departed so late, the couple requires hospitality to break their journey home for the night. The man refuses to stop at Jebus (Jerusalem), which was a foreign city at that stage. Instead, he chooses to journey on to Gilbeah or Ramah, which are Benjaminite towns, supposedly allies. Despite their waiting in the town square, however, they receive no offers of hospitality until an old man who comes from the same area as the Levite offers these words: "Peace be to you, I will care for all your wants; only do not spend the night in the square."

---

[14] Russell, *Just Hospitality*, 19.

When the men of the city demand that the host release the Levite so they can have sexual relations with him, the old man's reaction raises questions about who, between the Levite and the woman, he considers his real guest and who deserves to be cared for and protected. Before sacrificing the "concubine," he is even willing to sacrifice his virgin daughter. In the end, the Levite forces the "concubine" out to provide sexual hospitality to the Benjaminite men, who gang-rape her until she collapses. They then abandon her at the old man's door.

Some biblical scholars argue that this sorry tale is recorded as a reminder to the Israelites of why they were right to have moved from rule by judges to a monarchy. Others have argued that this story, like other equally horrific tales, should be excised from the canon because it does not reveal the saving grace of a loving God. We can only be repulsed by the Levite's subsequent actions. He takes the raped woman home (it is unclear whether she is dead or alive), dismembers her, and distributes her body parts throughout the land with the message: "Has such a thing ever happened since the Israelites were freed from Egypt? Consider it, take counsel, and speak out" (Judges 19:30). Contemporary readers share the outrage the Levite expressed in Judges 19:30 above.

The individual tragedy of the abused concubine is apparent, yet in the biblical narrative, male protagonists find excuses, prejudices, and political theories to keep them from accepting basic truths of human suffering. Tragedy fuels further tragedy as revenge and violence escalate and trauma compounds. In both the biblical and Rwandan stories, lack of justice for the individual women is most painful. Their bodies are wrecked by the careless greed of men, and the response from the women's kinsmen is shame, disgust, and further violence. The shame experienced by the victims fuels the conspiracy of silence that often surrounds such violent acts.

Reading this narrative through the interpretive lens of CBS helps break the silence and allows the story to be embodied in women who are current victims of sexual violence, including the Rwandan woman depicted at the beginning of this article, and myself. It also helps name the violation itself and its implication, with the hope that such awareness raising can lead to a mobilization for justice and change.

Since the ecumenical decade of churches in solidarity with women (1988–98), which was an ecclesial response to the United Nations' decade of women (1976–85), the Women in Black in Israel and Palestine were already breaking the silence by naming rape as a weapon of war in conflict situations. From their resistance, together with the Thursday protests by the Mothers of the Plaza de Mayo in Argentina and other women's campaigns and praxis resisting violence against women and violence in general, the World Council of Churches launched a global campaign known as Thursdays in Black for a world without rape and violence.

Enhancing the intersectional approach to addressing oppression, black in this campaign is used as a color of resistance. Every Thursday, the global community is invited to wear black in peaceful resistance against rape as blasphemous to the God who created humanity, female and male, in God's image and resistance to violence in general, thus building a global movement that scandalizes sexual and gender-based violence as well as violence as a whole, opting for a culture of gender justice and peace. Many member churches and faith-based organizations—for example, the Christian AIDS Bureau of Southern Africa (CABSA),[15] World Federation of Methodists and Uniting Church Women,[16] and Church of Sweden—have adopted Thursdays in Black as part of their own "pilgrimages" for justice and peace.[17]

---

[15] CABSA, "Thursdays in Black: Toward a World without Rape and Violence," accessed February 9, 2017, http://www.thursdaysinblack.co.za/cabsa/.
[16] World Federation of Methodist and Uniting Women, "Thursdays in Black," accessed February 9, 2017, http://wfmucw.org/thursdays-in-black.
[17] Svenska Kyrkan, "Thursdays in Black," https://blogg.svenskakyrkan.se/opinion/why-thursdays-in-black/

This campaign is not a stand-alone response against sexual and gender-based violence; it works with many other initiatives. For example, three World Council of Churches (WCC) initiatives are working toward gender justice and peace: work with men and boys for transformative masculinities, the No Xcuse campaign together with the online 16 Days of Activism against sexual and gender-based violence, and the process of accompaniment of trafficked and sexually violated women and girls in their healing. The WCC started to involve men and boys in the process of transformative masculinities for mutual partnership with the acknowledgment that over 70percent of sexual and gender-based violence is directly caused by men. This exploration of the way men are socialized into the masculinities of domination and violence using narrative was a joint initiative with the World Communion of Reformed Churches as part of the process of the decade to overcome violence (2001–10) and the Accra Confession's dismantling patriarchal hegemony, respectively.

Since the decade to overcome violence, the WCC has been using the Christian calendar, especially the week of Lent, to provide a scheduled focus to addressing sexual and gender-based violence and as a call to those whom patriarchal hegemony privileges, to fast against such patriarchal privileges. With the Young Women's Christian Association (YWCA) and Lutheran World Federation (LWF), the WCC recorded messages from religious leaders that affirmed that there simply is no religious justification for violence against women. The WCC also invited members of the global faith-based community to join these sixteen days of activism (November 25–December 10 each year) by recording their own videos with such messages as "No Xcuse for violence against women."

Global statistics show that 80 percent of trafficked persons are women and children; 79 percent of these are turned into commodities of sexual exploitation. Several churches and faith-based communities are working to address this modern form of slavery, yet sometimes, even after trafficked women and children are rescued, these institutions have no clear plan to assist them in the healing process, and trauma may remain with them for the rest of their lives. From a feminist perspective, an ethic of care must be developed that holistically addresses trauma by creating safe spaces in which building a community of wounded healers can take place. After care guidelines are developed, a process of weaving those guidelines into the realities that women and girls face can contribute to the psychological and spiritual healing process.

Because for WCC member churches, the Bible is a major source of the theological ethical basis of such responses, reading Judges 19 through the interpretive lens of CBS is an important tool and strategy. Not only does it help raise awareness, but as a community-based process, CBS also helps challenge those communities to make visible the realities of sexual and gender-based violence within their milieu. In this essay, I described how my encounter with the desiccated body of a Rwandan woman who was gang-raped and murdered helped re-member the biblical narrative as well as my own story of sexual abuse at an early age. Such an integration of perspectives helps my own activism for gender justice and peace. As a theological ethicist who reads the Bible using CBS, I find that CBS helps raise awareness of and builds resistance against sexual and gender-based violence. It also challenges religious communities to place theologically based activism at the core of their missions.

We can change neither the Judges 19 narrative nor the story of the raped Rwandan woman; however, by reading these narratives using CBS, we can break the silence around sexual and gender-based violence and work toward a culture of justice and peace wherein women's and girls' bodies are respected and kept whole.

Selected Bibliography

Ali, Kecia. *Marriage and Slavery in Early Islam.* Cambridge, MA: Harvard University Press, 2010.

———. "Obedience and Disobedience in Islamic Discourses." In *Encyclopedia of Women in Islamic Cultures,* edited by Suad Joseph, 309-13. Leiden, Netherlands: Brill, 2007.

Bird, Jennifer G. "Ephesians." In *Fortress Commentary on the Bible: The New Testament,* edited by Margaret Aymer, Cynthia Briggs Kittredge, and David A. Sanchez, 527-42. Minneapolis, MN: Fortress, 2014.

Bowen, Nancy R. "Women, Violence, and the Bible." In *Engaging the Bible in a Gendered World: An Introduction to Feminist Biblical Interpretation in Honor of Katharine Doob Sakenfeld,* edited by Linda Day and Carolyn Pressler, 186-99. Louisville, KY: Westminster John Knox, 2006.

Brenner, Athalya. "Some Reflections on Violence against Women and the Image of the Hebrew God: The Prophetic Books Revisited." In *On the Cutting Edge: The Study of Women in Biblical Worlds: Essays in Honor of Elisabeth Schüssler Fiorenza,* edited by Jane Schaberg, Alice Bach, and Esther Fuchs, 69-81. New York: Continuum, 2004,.

Brock, Rita Nakashima. *Journeys by Heart: A Christology of Erotic Power.* New York: Crossroad, 1988.

Chaudhry, Ayesha S. *Domestic Violence and the Islamic Tradition: Ethics, Law, and the Muslim Discourse on Gender.* New York: Oxford University Press, 2013.

Claassens, L. Juliana M. "Calling the Keeners: The Image of the Wailing Woman as Symbol of Survival in the Traumatized World." *Journal of Feminist Studies in Religion* 26, no. 1 (2010): 63–77.

Day, Linda. "Rhetoric and Domestic Violence in Ezekiel 16." *Biblical Illustrator* 8, no. 3 (2000): 205–30.

Gravett, Sandie. "Reading 'Rape' in the Hebrew Bible: A Consideration of Language." *Journal for the Study of the Old Testament* 28, no. 3 (2004): 279–99.

Herman, Judith. *Trauma and Recovery: The Aftermath of Violence—from Domestic Abuse to Political Terror.* New York: Basic, 1992.

Hudson, Valerie M., Bonnie Ballif-Spanvill, Mary Caprioli, and Chad F. Emmett. *Sex and World Peace.* New York: Columbia University Press, 2012.

Scholz, Susanne. *Sacred Witness: Rape in the Hebrew Bible.* Minneapolis, MN: Fortress, 2010.

Schüssler Fiorenza, Elisabeth. "Ties that Bind: Violence against Wo/men." In *Transforming Vision: Explorations in Feminist The*logy,* 97–124. Minneapolis, MN: Fortress, 2011.

Townsley, Gillian. "The Straight Mind in Corinth: Problematizing Categories and Ideologies of Gender in 1 Corinthians 11:2–16." In *Bible Trouble: Queer Reading at the Boundaries of Biblical Scholarship,* edited by Teresa J. Hornsby and Ken Stone, 247–81. Atlanta, GA: Society of Biblical Literature, 2011.

Trible, Phyllis. *Texts of Terror: Literary-Feminist Readings of Biblical Narratives.* Minneapolis, MN: Fortress, 1984.

Washington, Harold C. "Violence and the Construction of Gender in the Hebrew Bible: A New Historicist Approach." *Biblical Illustrator* 5, no. 4 (1997): 324–63.

Weaver, Andrew, John D. Preston, and Charlene Hosenfeld. *Counseling on Sexual Issues: A Handbook for Pastors and Other Helping Professionals.* Cleveland, OH: Pilgrim, 2005.

Weems, Renita J. *Battered Love: Marriage, Sex, and Violence in the Hebrew Prophets.* Minneapolis, MN: Fortress, 1995.

Williams, Delores, "Black Women's Surrogate Experience and Christian Notions of Redemption." In *After Patriarchy: Feminist Transformations of the World Religions*, edited by Paula Cooey, William R. Eakin, and Jay B. McDaniel, 1–13. Maryknoll, NY: Orbis, 1991.

www.ingramcontent.com/pod-product-compliance
Lightning Source LLC
Chambersburg PA
CBHW050826160426
43192CB00010B/1910